The Essence of the
Reformation

INCLUDES BONUS CLASSIC WORKS
by Luther, Calvin and Cranmer

Kirsten Birkett

The Essence of the Reformation
Second edition
© Matthias Media 2009

First edition 1998

Matthias Media
(St Matthias Press Ltd ACN 067 558 365)
PO Box 225
Kingsford NSW 2032
Australia
Telephone: (02) 9663 1478; international: +61-2-9663-1478
Facsimile: (02) 9663 3265; international: +61-2-9663-3265
Email: info@matthiasmedia.com.au
Internet: www.matthiasmedia.com.au

Matthias Media (USA)
Telephone: 724 964 8152; international: +1-724-964-8152
Facsimile: 724 964 8166; international: +1-724-964-8166
Email: sales@matthiasmedia.com
Internet: www.matthiasmedia.com

ISBN 978 1 921441 33 2

Contents

Preface

Preface

There are millions of people alive today who believe what they believe because of what happened in Europe 500 years ago. The fights of the Reformation have shaped Protestant churches ever since. Christians who have been taught within those traditions are inheriting ideas that were formulated in the sixteenth century.

However, most Protestants today know very little about the earth-shattering events and debates of the Reformation. We casually recite words that cost people their lives when they were first uttered. And we take many ideas for granted that were once fiercely contested.

Why did the Reformers think their doctrinal ideas worth dying for? And do they still matter today?

When we study the Reformation, we are studying ourselves, for many of the same problems and confusions are alive and well in today's churches. History demonstrates what happens when wrong ideas flourish; if we know our history, we can learn what mistakes to avoid today.

Part I

What was religion like in medieval Europe?

When Christianity first spread across Europe during the sixth century, it came face to face with a variety of ancient pagan religions. The missionaries were often in danger, either rejected outright or asked to prove the greatness of their God in some contest against the pagan priest. How were they to deal with this? Should any compromise be made, or should all the trappings of pagan worship be denounced and destroyed?

In 601, Pope Gregory wrote on this matter to Abbot Mellitus in England:

> *To my most beloved son, Abbot Mellitus,*
> *[from] Gregory, servant of the servants of God.*
>
> *Since the departure of our companions and your-self I have felt much anxiety because we have not happened to hear how your journey has prospered. However, when Almighty God has brought you to our most reverent brother Bishop Augustine, tell him what I have decided after long deliberation about the English people, namely that the idol temples of that race should by no means be destroyed, but only the idols in them. Take holy water and sprinkle it in these shrines, build altars and place relics in them. For if the shrines are well built, it is essential that they should be changed from the worship of devils to the service of the true God. When this people see that their shrines are not destroyed they will be able to banish error from their hearts and be more ready*

to come to the places they are familiar with, but now recognizing and worshipping the true God. And because they are in the habit of slaughtering much cattle as sacrifices to devils, some solemnity ought to be given them in exchange for this. So on the day of the dedication or the festivals of the holy martyrs, whose

Pope Gregory

relics are deposited there, let them make themselves huts from the branches of trees around the churches which have been converted out of shrines, and let them celebrate the solemnity with religious feasts. Do not let them sacrifice animals to the devil, but let them slaughter animals for their own food to the praise of God, and let them give thanks to the Giver of all things for His bountiful provision. Thus while some outward rejoicings are preserved, they will be able more easily to share in inward rejoicings.

Pope Gregory followed the policy that the medieval church generally adopted—to ease the missionary process a little by allowing potential converts to keep some things they had previously venerated. For better or worse, it was decided that many pagan holy sites would survive, and be made into Christian places of worship.

This kind of background helps to explain how the medieval church came to be such a diverse and immense structure. It not only grew and developed over more than a thousand years, it also encompassed people of vastly different class and education, different native customs and regional traditions. What was taught by the local priest was commonly mixed with beliefs from the old religions, even though it all went under the same name.

Most European people in the middle ages were very religious; but what precisely they believed, and what it meant to them, is not necessarily found by studying official doctrine of the church fathers and the medieval universities. If we are to understand a little of what the Reformation accomplished, and the differences it made, we need a brief glance at some of the many different ways in which medieval religion operated.

1 Pagan beliefs and medieval religion

Where did medieval magic stop and medieval religion begin? The line was hard to draw. There was no doubt what the difference was in the mind of medieval theologians: magic was of the devil, and evil; whereas religion was of God. Whatever activity was not authorized by the church was magic, and therefore evil. In practice, however, the line became fuzzy, because church activities were often remarkably similar to those activities labeled magical; indeed, there was occasionally some confusion as to precisely which activities were to be condemned.

An example taken from the Anglo-Saxon church illustrates this confusion. Magical remedies, such as chanting charms, were clearly condemned. However, it was quite legitimate for monks at a shrine to wash the bones of a saint in water and then give the water to a patient to drink as a healing remedy. Even when the water was poured on the earth, the dust there when the water dried was held to have the same healing power. "No-one shall enchant a herb with magic", wrote Aelfric, an early medieval cleric, "but with God's word shall bless it, and so eat it". The guidebooks for priests about what to ask a confessor and what penances to give (called 'penitentials') taught a similar message: "Hast thou collected medicinal herbs with evil incantations, not with the creed and the Lord's prayer, that is, with the singing of the 'credo in Deum' and the paternoster?" This distinction—between 'evil incantations' and things such as the Lord's prayer—may sound quite plain until it is realized that most incantations *included* the Lord's prayer and blessings from God's word. In practice, magic and religion were very similar. In fact, it was not only the practices that were similar, but the world view that the practices were built on—namely, *that the supernatural interacted daily with the natural and could be manipulated, or at least affected, by words and ritual.* The medieval church condemned magic: but the church itself was tied up in the framework of thought that made magic possible, and so implicitly encouraged the practices it condemned.

How did this situation come about? After the New Testament era, Christianity began spreading into a world already occupied by a multitude of other religious beliefs and systems. Christianity came into sharp conflict with these other religions. As Christianity spread, pagan religions were denounced and condemned as demonic. However, the problem frequently arose of how to persuade pagans to transfer their allegiance from their traditional pagan gods to the Christian one. Often the evangelistic process came down to a battle of power, a contest of the miracles of the evangelist against the powers of the pagan priest. For instance, it is told that Alban, an early English saint, miraculously parted the waters of a stream on the way to his execution and then caused a spring to appear at his feet as he stood about to be beheaded. Unfortunately for Alban, he was beheaded nonetheless, but his executioner immediately and miraculously lost his eyes and the local ruler ordered persecution of Christians to cease.

As history shows, frequently the Christian mission-aries must have been victorious, for Christianity did indeed spread throughout Europe with remarkable speed. The Christian God had triumphed over pagan gods, which gave the church authority to denounce paganism and forbid the worship of its gods. However, the very nature of the miracle contests meant that the idea of supernatural power available in the world was reinforced. Technically, the missionaries may have been only God's instruments, unable to control the power God gave them, or even to determine whether he would give it: but in practice, they appeared as stronger magicians. Also, the contests demonstrated that although the pagan gods may have been defeated, they were still there. The medieval church had gained dominance as a stronger religion, but not an essentially different religion from the more magical faiths it was replacing.

What is more, pagan culture and even religion was frequently not destroyed, but assimilated. Probably the most famous example of this policy is seen in the letter that begins this chapter, in which Pope Gregory advises Abbot Mellitus to tolerate pagan practices for the sake of peaceful relations with the new converts and an easier transition for them into Christianity.

This approach led to the existence of holy wells, which were previously magical wells connected with pagan worship. It also led to pagan festivals becoming Christian: the celebration of the winter solstice, which became Christmas; the spring fertility rites that were turned into Easter.

It was not that pagan religion was approved of—medieval penitentials show much evidence of outright rejection of paganism and its ceremonies. "If anyone makes, or releases from, a vow beside trees or springs or by a lattice, or anywhere except in a church, he shall do penance for three years on bread and water, since this is sacrilege or a demonic thing", declares one medieval penitential. Worshipping the moon or the stars was specifically condemned. Taking offerings to a pagan site was out of the question.

Despite these examples, there was a deliberate inclusion of much from paganism, which broadened Christian doctrine considerably and significantly affected its practice. Some historians argue that far from this process of inclusion being a weakness or carelessness on the part of the medieval church, it was a careful policy of assimilation, part of a plan enabling the church to survive and expand in a diverse culture. That is, confrontation with paganism could only go so far: in order to win the battle, the church also took the ground away from the 'enemy' by taking over magical elements of paganism and transforming them into an acceptable form. Thus the medieval church became a channel of supernatural power into the world, and was moreover able to establish itself as the only legitimate means of doing so. The church could not realistically destroy magic; it divided magic into the legitimate and the illegitimate, and transformed the legitimate into religion. It was a successful policy, and the church came to dominate European life. Unfortunately, it also meant that the church began to bear an increasingly poor resemblance to the biblical Christianity taught by Christ and his apostles.

There are numerous examples of magical elements of pagan religion being incorporated into Christian thought and popular devotion. The pre-Christian evil *daimones*, for example, who were creatures of the air with divinatory powers, were renamed demons. Their assaults upon men, and temptations to wickedness, made them helpful scapegoats for moral failings. The discrepancy between the moral ideals of the monks and their real-life failings was explained by demonic assault, and in fact the monastic life began to be portrayed as a war against demons.

Angels, similarly, were to some extent the good daimones 'rescued' and brought into medieval orthodoxy. Augustine discusses whether Plato's 'daemones' might be the same as scriptural angels.[1] They were also 'aery' beings, with bodies far superior to man and even superior to the demons. As such, they were effective supernatural allies against the magic of the demons. They had greater powers of foresight than demons, for the angels knew the wisdom of God. Saints could call upon angels to counter the plagues and pestilences supposedly created by demons. This good Christian supernatural power, then, could over-

1. *The City of God*, IX chapter 23.

come the bad demonic magic. Augustine claimed that it was angels who enabled Moses and Aaron to defeat Pharoah's magicians.[2]

2 Sacraments and priests

The medieval church became part of the lives of people through public rituals and ceremonies, which both expressed and reinforced its role as spiritual authority. It is hard to overestimate the influence that the church had on medieval life. All life was religious. Virtually all people were baptized and therefore considered Christian and part of the church. Church life was based on the sacraments: definite, obvious activities in which everyone participated. The seven sacraments that had developed by the late Middle Ages—baptism, the eucharist (the Mass), marriage, ordination, confirmation, confession and final unction—provided the framework of the daily work of the church and were vitally important cultural rites in any person's life.

The eucharist, or Mass, was practised throughout the Middle Ages, but it was not until the eleventh century that many of its basic theological issues began to be sorted out. It was around this time that debates over the meaning of *hoc est corpus meum* ('this is my body') began in earnest. This debate was

2.   *The City of God*, X chapter 8.

more than just an argument about the Lord's Supper and how it was to be celebrated. It was tied up with heavyweight philosophical debates about the nature of all reality—whether, for example, there truly were universals that represented the true forms of things on earth, or whether universal categories of things only existed as constructs of our minds. The philosophy of Aristotle was much in favour in this period, and his theory of matter was particularly important for discussion about the Mass. Aristotle taught that the form (or external characteristics) of an object was distinct from its substance (its inner essence), and so theoretically it was possible for the inner substance of something to change while its outward properties appeared to be unaffected. This philosophical point is the essence of the doctrine of transubstantiation, which arose in the twelfth century.

Transubstantiation taught that the 'substance' of the bread changed into the real body of Christ during the Mass even though its outward form remained unchanged. The visible outward part of the ceremony was considered a sign that was separate from the spiritual reality that lay behind it. It was never taught officially that the sign alone could do anything. However, the sign was still totally necessary for the spiritual reality to reach people. The bread *was* Christ's very body. The teaching of transubstantiation emphasized that the body of Christ, and nothing else, was present in every bit of the bread and wine. As Stephen Gardiner, Bishop of Winchester, said during the debates of the Reformation: "Present he is, and truly is, and verily is, and so in deed, that is to say, really is, and unfeignedly is, and therefore in substance is, and, as we term it, substantially is present".

Transubstantiation was by no means accepted at once by the theological elite: indeed, acceptance of the doctrine depended heavily on the theologian's philosophy of nature. By the end of the fifteenth century there was still controversy. However, these were arguments of the theological elite, a very small percentage of the population. From the twelfth century, it was accepted in ordinary church life that the bread became the real body of Christ.

By the mid-twelfth century, the eucharist was considered to be the most important of all the sacraments. It could never be given by a lay person. Diocesan regulations began to include such things as instructions on how to make the bread. Also, the physical 'host' (as the bread was called) began to be guarded carefully. A cloth had to be held under the chins of recipients so no crumbs would drop to the floor. The host would be locked up, both before and after the ceremony. Very costly vessels would be made to contain the host. (The wine never gained the same importance.) The eucharistic ritual gradually came to take the shape that it would hold for centuries after, with practices such as elevation (lifting the bread so everyone could see it), ringing bells and lighting candles. Also, from the twelfth century, teaching about the suffering of souls after death in purgatory provided the framework for what would become a very common practice—the saying of Masses for the dead. Whether or not these Masses really helped the dead was debated in theological circles, but in the daily teaching there was no doubt.

The Mass, then, became part of regular local community life. Guidebooks and pamphlets were distributed to teach the significance of the eucharist in each parish. Texts were written in the common language, and the most popular were the stories illustrating the power of the eucharist in daily life. The Mass was an activity that united the local community.

Many accounts of visions were spread in order to shock heretics into realizing the truth of the miracle of the Mass. The host was said to change into a bleeding child, or a child with five wounds, or pieces of flesh, or similar gruesome sights. Such visions would convince the disbeliever that though the host looked like bread, it genuinely changed into the flesh of Christ at the consecration. Miracle stories circulated in which animals would recognize the host and bow to it. Similar stories were reflected in illustrations showing a priest raising a child to heaven. The elevation of the host was the primary way in which lay people participated in the ritual, and the supernatural power inherent in Christ's body was thereby transferred to communicants. Blessings simply flowed out from the host.

It is hardly surprising, then, that as well as 'official' teaching concerning the Mass, many other popular beliefs sprang up. Theologians insisted the host was not to be treated as magical, but in practice it was. The bread was widely believed to have healing powers: it could be stolen by keeping it in the mouth without swallowing, then used as medicine or as a protective amulet for the person, crops, livestock or house. Attending the Mass was thought to cure illness. Whooping cough could be cured by drinking from the chalice after Mass. The priestly teaching only emphasized the power of the Mass by the emphasis it placed on the dreadful supernatural punishments that came upon people who abused it.

The Mass was the central part of medieval religion, but the other sacraments also shaped the way people viewed Christianity. Baptism was an essential rite in people's lives. The water was exorcised and the salt blessed, and they would be used with ritual words to force the devil to depart from the child. The water had to be locked up to prevent it from being stolen and used in superstitious rites. The cloth tied over the child's forehead was to be burned or kept by the priest for the use of the church. Holy water in general was thought to have power to cast out demons and drive away disease.

The priesthood also supported the church's claim to supernatural power. The priest was not merely better educated and a full-time church worker; he was considered supernaturally different, of a different order from lay people. He had access to knowledge and power unavailable to others: only he could say the words that transformed bread into flesh and blood; only he was able to touch the host. Augustine wrote that at ordination a priest received a spiritual character, not from the ordaining minister but from Christ himself. This indelible power made it possible for even a bad priest to administer the sacraments, for it was Christ who acted in the ceremonies the priest performed.

Apart from the sacraments, many other ceremonies of the church shaped the understanding of how Christians were to have daily contact with the power of the spiritual realms. The consecrating of churches was to give them a kind of supernatural protection. The Feast of Candlemas included the blessing of candles that were given out to parishioners for protection against evil forces. Holy Week culminated in the procession of Palm Sunday in which the host, the 'real body' of Jesus, was carried into the church; and it was believed that crosses made during the reading of the gospels had healing powers. A loaf of bread, presented by a parishioner at the end of the parish Mass, was blessed and distributed to the congregation; the bread was believed to have powers of protection. Sacred things had the power to banish the devil; holy water had 'effectual power' to cast out demons and drive away disease. The name and cross of Christ had inexorable power. Blessed salt, water and wax were *intended* for the use of the laity as protection. They could cure animals, drive away demons and help women in labour. The Rogationtide ceremony, in which clergy and parishioners walked around the fields, gave fertility to the coming season's crops.

The medieval church also believed in the supernatural power of words, seen in attitudes to the Bible. Paradoxically, it was because of a belief in the inherent power of words that the church resisted translating the Bible from Latin into the common tongue. The argument was that the words themselves, as recorded, had to be preserved. So even when translation was allowed by the Catholic church in the second half of the sixteenth century, some theologians insisted on almost exact correspondence between the translation and the original—frequently leading to unintelligible translations. Many Latin words were kept, and sometimes the words of Christ in performing miracles were left in Aramaic. This attitude to the Bible could also be seen in church ceremony. Gospel texts were thought to be powerful as the collection of particular letters, quite apart from their actual message. Books of the Gospels were kissed and venerated. Also, the Latin liturgy was considered to be powerful in the same way as the Bible, both coming from God, and conveying power to those who used them *even if their meaning was not understood*. Latin primers were extremely popular and frequently 'read' by a population who could not possibly have known all of the meaning of the prayers included. Indeed, many of the prayers included in primers called upon the power of strange words for protections against sickness and danger.

3 Saints and miracles

Further examples of the world view of medieval religion are found in the cults of saints and beliefs about miracles.

The cult of the saints started with Christians who merely wished to remember and honour their martyrs in the early days of the church. Christians were willing to associate themselves with the dead, which was in strong contrast to pagan superstitions concerning death. The tomb of a martyr saint was a meeting place between earth and heaven: the saint was in heaven, in the presence of God, but also tied to the tomb where physical relics—bones and so on—began to have more importance. In such a meeting place it became reasonable to expect miracles to occur. By the fifth century, healing miracles were well established and began to be advertised. Purification rituals were introduced, all designed to heighten the sense of awe

Remains of St Alban's shrine

surrounding the relics. The relics were elevated and took on even more of an aura of holiness.

The shrines of the saints were not just thought of as a place for miracles; they were meant to be a place where God could be worshipped through the saint. However, healing miracles at the tombs were expected and celebrated. Some efforts were made to test the reality of the miracles and keep accurate records, though of course the loyalties of the shrine monks who kept such records would undoubtedly have coloured their memories.

By the sixteenth century, pilgrimages to healing shrines in England were very frequent. Some saints were famous for healing particular illnesses; others were associated with a particular locality and were known to protect their own district. Also, there were many individual shrines to the virgin Mary. The process of becoming a saint was a long and often very expensive one for the champions of a saint, and miracles that had been performed by the candidate while alive came to be very important as evidence of their holiness. So the biographies of saints' lives developed as a major form of literature, often describing supernatural power in the daily life of a saint.

4 Why the change?

We now begin to have a more accurate picture of what medieval religion was like. Religion was very important to the people of pre-Reformation Europe. Traditional Catholicism was a central and basic part of community and individual lives. Pilgrimage to the tombs of saints was, if anything, on the increase in the fifteenth century. Religious literature was tremendously popular, and religious education of lay people had been improving, especially after the invention of the printing press. Pre-Reformation religion was strong, lively, and held a great power in the community, in the ordinary beliefs and loyalties of the people. Popular religious movements were many, seeking a holier and simpler lifestyle. There was certainly corruption in the political activities of the church, but we should not think that dislike of the corruption meant that the church was losing adherents on a wide scale, or that the church was in any danger of internal collapse. The fact that so many of the laity did object to the corruption is in some sense evidence of their commitment to the church as an institution.

The kind of corruption that existed was mainly to do with the opportunities for making money in the church hierarchy. There were many grievances against the Pope, or church management in general. One was that the Pope had by the sixteenth century considerable power to appoint archbishops, bishops and abbots as well as other clerical offices. This was financially beneficial for the Pope, for not only did a fee have to be paid by the appointee of up to one year's income, but while the office was vacant all revenue went to the Pope. The Pope also had under his authority the disciplinary mechanism of 'reservation of sins'—certain sins that required his forgiveness. The sinner who had committed these deeds (such as certain crimes against church property) was required to pay for special forgiveness. Excommunication was another threat the Pope and his bishops could wield against anyone who resisted the many taxes and fees that were levied upon clergy and church activities. The fact that so many church benefits were effectively for sale was a source of widespread anger. The rich could manage to have their family members appointed to influential church positions, regardless of whether they were qualified. Many church rules could be set aside for individuals who paid the right fee. Moreover, although marriage was denied to the clergy, keeping a concubine was possible and even accepted for some.

This disparity between a desire for genuine religious life on the part of simple people, and the decaying political games of the church hierarchy, became a great source of stress. The church was not providing what people anxious for salvation wanted. While there were no doubt many people who were quite happy with a system that merely required them to keep up ritual observances, there were also many who rejected the emptiness of a ritual show provided by a financially-driven institution.

What did the Reformation do for these people? Organizationally, the Reformation overturned many social injustices and corruptions in the church hierarchy. These changes most lay people welcomed. *Theologically*, however, the Reformation was to a large extent the re-evangelization of an essentially pagan Europe. There had been popular movements of change in earlier centuries that had tried to challenge existing beliefs, such as the Lollards in England. Survivors of these movements provided at least a portion of the population who already had some grounding in the new message. For many, however, they were hearing the message of biblical Christianity for the first time. Some saw it as a challenge to old established rituals that provided a familiar framework of stability in a harsh world, and so resisted. Others viewed it as a new message of hope and liberation, in which God, who was more powerful than any evil, could be reached without the intercession of saint or priest.

Before we consider what this message of liberation was—and its implications—let us turn to the details of what actually happened.

Part II

What happened where?

1 Germany

The Reformation began in Germany. It is interesting to consider whether this really matters. After all, Martin Luther was an inspiring and inspired man, who was convinced of the truth of the Christian gospel and was determined to preach it. Did it make any difference where he was?

It probably did. Although it was Luther who set the Reformation moving, Germany was a particularly receptive place for his message. The political conditions, social structure and recent events all provided fertile ground for a movement of revolt against the established church.

a) Political conditions

We should note that there was actually no such thing as 'Germany' in the sixteenth century; there were German-speaking territories of the Holy Roman Empire. (We will use 'Germany' as a convenient shorthand.) The Holy Roman Empire was the descendant of the Roman Empire, and the emperor was elected from the ranks of the powerful. Although the emperor nominally had control over most of Europe, there was no central government, bureaucracy or army—just what the emperor himself could provide.

Consequently, German cities had a great deal of political independence, and people had greater freedom of movement than did those in many other sixteenth-century countries. German cities and princes were only theoretically under the power of the emperor. For the most part it was not in the interests of the princes to have a strong emperor, as their power would decrease under a strong overlord. These conditions help us to understand, in part, why Luther's religious dissent was able to spread so rapidly, even though the Emperor Charles V was against him. This emperor was very popular, perhaps the most popular emperor for centuries, but he could not force his subordinates to obey him. Also, many of the princes were indecisive and so did not prevent the ideas from spreading. For the most part, the only principalities that followed the Emperor, and took steps to stop Luther's ideas from spreading, were those controlled by bishops.

The bishops had a great deal of power; the church was a political body, as well as a religious one. Bishops could be, in effect, independent territorial rulers, as powerful as princes. The abbeys, one level down, were also rich and powerful, ruled by prince-abbots. The bishops and abbots, like any other princes, wanted to extend their territories. At the same time, because these church positions did carry a lot of power, members of the noble houses tried to be appointed to them for their own advancement, and most high church officials were also nobility.

Germans, however, had to compete with foreigners for these choice situations. Italian favourites at the papal court were strong contenders, which did nothing to increase the popularity of Rome with Germans. Most levels of German society could have done without church rule altogether. Since well before the Reformation, there had been agitation to see the church come under secular control. The major problem was that clergy were not answerable to secular courts, but church courts could try lay-people even on non-spiritual matters. There was a great deal of resentment against the church. Throughout the fifteenth century, it was a common complaint that Germany had to escape the power of Rome, and even create an independent German church.

b) Social conditions and events

The social conditions in Germany also prepared the way for the Reformation. Around the beginning of the sixteenth century, the German states experienced enormous problems of order and public peace, which their rulers were largely unable to control. The countryside was plagued with banditry and feud. Trade was disrupted by the lack of any uniform coinage or excise system. Justice was hampered by the fact that there was no efficient legal system. Positions of power were fought over. Many of the nobility considered themselves above the law. There was no authority to settle disputes or to enforce agreed terms. Illegal acts within the church, and outside it, could take place with no fear of legal retribution.

At the same time, German universities had been flourishing. The numbers of people with university education had risen considerably in the century before the Reformation. However, the number of jobs did not increase at the same rate; so there was a large number of people with intellectual talent, discontented with the opportunities available, and fed up with a system riddled with pluralism, favouritism, simony (church positions for sale) and foreign (Roman) control.

Another important cultural event was the invention of printing. Not only would this become a superb tool for Luther to spread his ideas, it had already had an impact on German religious life. The printing trade was religious from the beginning, and was used to promote religious knowledge. Some bishops had used the printing press to better educate their clergy, and even lay people. Luther's ideas reached people who were already used to religious discussion through printed literature. Through his emotional and forceful writing, Luther was able to make people seriously concerned about their salvation—concerned enough to throw off the shackles of the Roman church. The theological ideas interested the intelligentsia, which made the Reformation a theological debate, not just a social movement. So much of the dispute occurred through publications, it is hard to imagine what the Reformation would have been without printing technology.

c) Luther

Germany was primed for a Reform movement; Luther provided the spark. But how did one monk manage to capture the hearts of the German people? The humble lecturer of theology in Wittenberg probably would not have struck anyone as the potential leader of a world-changing movement. Luther certainly did not think of himself as one; he was thoroughly caught up with the problem of his own salvation. Luther came to understand that salvation was by faith alone, not by religious works. It was a radical message, but initially it appears that Luther intended to do no more with it than teach it to his students as correct theology.

Martin Luther was the son of a miner in Saxony. He showed early intellectual promise, and was sent to study; but by his own inclination he became an Augustinian monk. He was soon appointed a professor at Wittenberg, and spent ten years there struggling with deep thoughts in the search for salvation.

Luther followed the rules of his order strictly, confessing for hours on end in his efforts to make sure every sin was accounted for. "I went into the cloister that I might not be lost but might have eternal life", he wrote. "The sight of a crucifix was like lightning to me and when his name was spoken I would rather have heard that of the devil, because I thought I must do good works until Christ, because of them, became friendly and gracious to me." He realized, however, he could never confess enough, or do

Martin Luther

penance enough, to cover his entire soul. The discipline of a monk's life, although it was as severe as he could make it, did not give him salvation.

Through study of the Bible, Luther came to realize that the gospel was not what the church had taught him. The Bible confirmed his conviction that humans are utterly sinful and deserve only to be condemned. Contrary to what he had been taught, however, he discovered that Christ offers free forgiveness to the sinner.

Luther did not immediately reject the Roman church. On the contrary, he intended to be an obedient servant, teaching theology from the Bible. Luther did not regard this theology as revolutionary (except personally), since it was present in the writings of the church fathers. Nevertheless, even if Luther did not recognize it himself at first, his doctrine of personal helplessness before God undermined the whole activity of the church.

What persuaded Luther to act was an especially sordid abuse of church authority—the sale of Indulgences. Indulgences were pardons from purgatory, the place where souls were thought to suffer after death to work off some of the punishment for their sins. Although initially Indulgences were very carefully used, in effect they meant that an individual could buy his way out of sin. For money, the sinner could have a guarantee of reduced time in purgatory without the tedious burden of doing penance. Germany became a site for widespread abuse of this system.

The local perpetrator was the Archbishop of Mainz, Albert of Hohenzollern. He had laid out a great deal of money for the purchase of several bishoprics. Indeed, he needed to pay for permission to become a bishop at all, as he was not legally old enough. Buying the powerful See of Mainz, which gave him ecclesiastical control over all Germany, left him deep in debt. To help him repay this debt, the Pope allowed him to sell Indulgences, with one half of the proceeds to go to Rome for the building of the new St Peter's Basilica.

In Luther's opinion, not only was the sale of Indulgences an abuse of power, but it denied the very heart of biblical theology. How could credit in heaven be bought? Luther, among others, challenged this practice. On 30 October 1517, Luther nailed his famous theses on the door of the Castle Church at Wittenberg. Such complaints were not unusual or particularly offensive, as they were used as a basis for debate, and Luther intended no more than that. He had not counted on the fact that his complaint actually went to the heart of the existence of the church at all. In essence, Luther argued that it was ridiculous to suppose that 'extra' grace could be bought. It was impossible that one person could be good enough to have grace left over to pass on to another, less perfect person. How could the church, then, ever build up a kind of bank of grace that could then be sold? Biblically, Luther was quite correct. He had not yet, however, drawn the conclusion that if this is true, then the whole system of church ceremony, which was designed to dispense grace to the participant, was empty. Other theologians were not so slow to see where Luther's complaints were leading. Luther was in trouble.

At first, it seems, Luther expected that reasonable discussion would resolve the problems. The hatred and suspicion he had stirred up, however, diminished his hopes. Over the next few years, opposition to Luther grew, culminating in excommunication by the Pope. The secular German authorities, however, were not quick to give him up. They were keen to end Italian dominion over Germany, and so Luther's insistence that the papacy was wrong was a welcome message. In 1518, Luther was summoned to Rome, but his prince, Frederick, managed to have the hearing transferred to Augsburg. To Luther's surprise, these talks were quite friendly; he had expected to be burned at the stake.

Luther returned to Wittenberg, and in 1519 held a famous disputation with the theologian John Eck. This did not go so well. Eck was a more experienced debater, and managed to manoeuvre Luther into being unmistakably heretical according to the current doctrine of the Roman church. It put Luther in greater danger, but it also showed him that he may as well throw himself wholeheartedly into this so-called heresy. From there on, Luther attacked the whole basis of the papacy and the sacraments of the church. He was formally excommunicated in June 1520. (Luther publicly burned this notice at Wittenberg.) Luther had by now become a fierce attacker of the church he at first only intended to assist, and the unwitting leader of a German revolutionary movement. The Emperor Charles V finally took notice of him. Luther was summoned with promise of safe conduct to the Diet (a sort of German national parliament) at the city of Worms in January 1521. The first thing Luther was asked, without any chance to present his argument, was to acknowledge his writings and deny his heretical doctrines. Luther asked for time

Luther testifying before the Diet of Worms

to consider, and Charles gave him twenty-four hours. Luther reappeared on the next day, confidently acknowledged his works, and stated that he stood by all his doctrines. It is at this point that the story has him say, "Here I stand; I can do no other".

Luther was outlawed, but his safe-conduct still stood. His friends took him out of Germany to Warburg, where he lived in hiding under the name 'Sir George'. Suddenly, he was removed from the fury and turmoil he had lived in for years; he was secluded, with nothing to do. Depression grasped him. However, he turned his leisure time to priceless use; he began to translate the Bible into German.

The Reformation movement continued without Luther, but things were beginning to get out of hand. Not all reforming preachers had Luther's grasp of theology, or his concern for order and peace. It was not difficult for radicals to find an audience among those angry with foreign and church dominion. This was the beginning of what is known as the radical Reformation, from which came the Anabaptists. Some of its leaders were religious madmen, spouting apocalyptic prophecy and preaching violence and impossible lifestyles. Some were more serious, as determined as Luther but concerned that he had not gone far enough. This more radical movement had no friends at all. Rome hated them as rebels, and the Lutherans hated them as radicals who were bringing the gospel into disrepute. The groups formed mainly in the country, but even in Wittenberg some extremes of anti-church behaviour began to be committed.

Luther returned to Wittenberg. There, his presence quelled the more violent acts. However, Luther was not able to control the behaviour of all Germany. His message had been one of rebellion against church authorities; it was a simple step for some of his hearers to demand justice from *all* authorities. The peasants of Germany had suffered under an unjust system for some time, and were ready for riot. The idea of freedom from oppression—not just from ecclesiastical landlords, but from all landlords—stirred up long-simmering resentments. The most radical agitators added to the problem with their preaching of apocalyptic prophecies. The Peasants' War began.

It was not much of a war. The peasants were a rioting mob, but not an army. Their sheer numbers overwhelmed several castles and churches, and they destroyed most of what they took. However, they had little organization or weaponry, and their main force was destroyed in 1525. The war was over in less than a year, and the peasants met with an even greater brutality than they had been protesting against.

In 1531, some level of political stability was reached for the Protestant cities of Germany. They formed a confederacy, the Schmalkaldic League, and became a reasonable-sized European power. This was no longer a religious protest; indeed, for many of the princes, it never had been purely or even centrally about religion. The league allowed independence from the Pope and the Emperor. Meanwhile, the Emperor had other problems. France had contested his supremacy, and allied itself with the Pope. The Emperor was at war on several fronts; a war that he eventually won. In 1527, he had invaded Rome and now had the Pope under his power. However, he had little time or resources to spare for the Protestant league. Even the Catholic princes in Germany had their hands full with the threat of Turkish invasion from Hungary. The Lutheran principalities therefore had some time to organize themselves.

Luther continued to clarify his doctrinal reforms,

44

and make suggestions for the living of a Christian life. It took several years from 1525-1530 for his doctrinal ideas to be codified. In 1530, the Augsburg confession was settled upon as the broad basis of the Lutheran churches. It had largely been the work of Philip Melanchthon, Luther's co-worker and theological partner. By the time of Luther's death (1546), there was an independent, Protestant church.

Luther's writing was always going to work against his desire for peace. He was an ardent soul, and wrote with the passion that stirred him. However, his constant use of violent and offensive language did not sit well with the image of an order-loving, peaceful reformer. At least, no-one believed him to desire peace; it was all too easy to see him as a vengeful, bloodthirsty rebel, and his reputation suffered because of it.

However, it is possible that Luther knew exactly what he was doing. He saw Christendom in a desperate state, and the more the church opposed his reasonable protests, the more he realized that simple diplomacy was not going to shake the complacent power of a corrupt ecclesiastical authority. At the same time, he knew that civil war was not the answer. Luther spent his life walking a very stressful tightrope. It was necessary to wake up the people to oppose the unjust system they were living with, but he also had to guide that enthusiasm in useful directions. With all the deep tensions, conflicts, personal ambitions and long-held grudges in Germany, it is amazing that Luther was able to create a doctrinally-reformed, cohesive Protestant church at all.

After the decisive political and doctrinal break with Rome, there were still thousands of problems to be resolved. When monks left their monasteries, what authority were they now under, and how were they to earn a living? Who was to manage the lands confiscated from the church? What was to be done with the money bequeathed for Masses to be said for the dead? The whole social and legal structure of Germany was affected. In a time when women had little financial security apart from marriage, nuns who left their convents were particularly vulnerable. Luther realized he could solve the problem for one of them, and married (ex-Sister) Catherine. Money from church lands was also used to provide dowries for ex-nuns, which was at the time necessary for them to find a decent marriage.

Luther ended his life in illness, and died a natural death. The soul-searching young monk had become a father, leader and mentor of his own family and of a country.

2 Switzerland

a) Zwingli

Soon after Luther began his campaign in Germany, the city of Zurich in Switzerland found itself with a similar agitator. Huldrych Zwingli, a priest at the city's Grossmunster Church from 1518, became convinced of biblical doctrines and began to teach others of them. He had a broader focus than Luther, being determined to combine ecclesiastical with social reform. He and Luther also differed in their views about the Eucharist. Zwingli was the first to declare that the bread and the wine were nothing more than simple bread and wine, which reminded Christians of Christ's death and stimulated faith in Christ's promises.

Zwingli soon gathered a following, and quite a number of influential opponents. Unlike Luther, however, his early path was relatively painless. The city council gave him permission to argue his views in a public disputation on 19 January 1523. Zwingli won; it was as simple as that. There was overwhelming agreement that he was right, and the church wrong. This was not totally unprecedented; in the century preceding the Reformation, the city council had already taken steps against monastic and ecclesiastical privilege. Subsequently, at Easter 1525, the Mass was abolished, and images removed. Soon afterwards, pilgrimages and saints' days were also abolished, and the communal poor relief was reformed. More courageously, the city refused to renew a treaty with the King of France concerning mercenary service.

Zurich thus provided a lead that other Swiss cities—Berne, and later Basel and Schaffhausen—

followed. Because in Switzerland the cities acted as territorial lords over the surrounding countryside, once the message had convinced the city it was spread throughout the whole area. Several cities staunchly resisted the message; it failed in Lucerne, Fribourg and Solothurn.

In Berne, a small but influential Reformation movement began in 1522. The city councillors evaded the bishop and took matters into their own hands. They held a disputation and decided that the reforming priest Georg Brunner was preaching according to the Scriptures. The movement grew under the leadership of the painter, writer and politician Nikolaus Manuel (1484-1530) and the Reformer Berchtold Haller (1492-1536). In 1527, pressure from the city's artisans led to the holding of another disputation. This took place in January 1528, and led to the official introduction of the Reformation within the city and its extended territory.

Zurich was also surging ahead with its reform programme. However, once started, as Wittenberg had demonstrated, public fervour was difficult to control. From 1523, there was considerable turmoil in and outside the city. People indulged in iconoclasm (the smashing of altars, statues and church art)—which does not always indicate mere rioting, but can come from a deep conviction and anger at false religious practices. Nonetheless, by 1524 the trouble in Zurich merged with the beginnings of the Peasants' War. The city council was still firmly for reform. After another series of disputations, the city authorities ordered the removal of all images from the churches. Even all organs were destroyed in 1527.

Some of the rural population was even more zealous, expecting other reforms such as the abolition of the tithe (no-one ever likes taxes). The most radical of them joined the Anabaptists. By 1524, a number of Swiss cities had begun to gather in opposition to Zurich and its ally, Berne. By 1529, a religious war between the Protestant and Romanist territories of Switzerland was inevitable.

To understand what happened in this conflict, the basis of Swiss politics needs to be taken into consideration. Switzerland at that time was a confederation of territories linked by a network of treaties. The government was collective, rather than centralized. That is, the stability of Switzerland rested on the agreement of all the member states to remain peaceful; there was no central force to maintain peace.

Afraid of the disintegration of the country, then, peace was the overriding concern of the states. The first confrontation was resolved peacefully, with the First Peace of Kappel of 1529; this was followed by the Second Peace in 1531. In contrast with the bloodshed of other countries, this may have seemed a great victory for the gospel. However, things are rarely so simple. The agreed peace in fact stifled the advance of Protestantism. When advance was attempted, two short battles in October 1531 decided the issue. Swiss Protestantism was defeated and Zwingli and many of Zurich's leaders died in battle. From then on, Protestants had to stay within their states, and so peace was maintained.

The agreement not only stopped the spread of the Reformation, it also stopped the growth of Switzerland, for taking in any new states would upset the balance between Protestant and Catholic territories. The only place where the Reformation in Switzerland did not stop in 1531 was at its very edges, with the states that did not have full membership of the confederacy.

It was mainly French-speaking Switzerland that took on the Reformation from the 1530s. The preacher Guillaume Farel (1489-1565) in Geneva helped prepare the ground. Under the city of Berne's protection, Farel began religious renewal from 1532, and managed to recruit John Calvin (1509-1564) to the cause.

b) Calvin

Calvin was born in France, and studied Latin and theology at the University of Paris, as well as studying law at Orleans. He was twenty-six years younger than Luther, and so grew up in a world where the Reformation was already a reality. By the time he reached adulthood, Western Christendom had been broken in

PROMPTE   ET SINCERE·

IOHANNES·CALVINVS·
ANNO·ÆTATIS·53·
·B·

John Calvin

two, and a Protestant church with Protestant theology existed. When Calvin began to be dissatisfied with the faith he was taught as a French Catholic, the alternative was ready at hand. He did not have to go through the same sort of anguished soul-searching that plagued Luther; when Calvin made his well thought out and soul-felt decision to renounce error, he was able to move fairly smoothly into Protestantism.

This careful and determined use of his intellectual gifts was to characterize Calvin for most of his life. While he had his share of persecution, physical insecurity and public controversy, he was able to bring to bear a remarkable mind with an intense godly conviction. It was in 1533 that he became thoroughly convicted of God's omnipotence and considered himself bound to proclaim the truth—a conviction he followed through for the rest of his life. He never seemed to waver with doubt, or go through the emotional extremes of a more passionate soul like Luther. He seriously applied himself to the difficult task before him, and did it.

Not long after his conversion in 1533, at the university in Paris where Calvin was now working, the rector preached a sermon with clearly Lutheran elements. In the outrage that followed, Calvin stood by the rector. The French king, Francis I, who was at this time trying to arrange a marriage between his son Henry and the Pope's niece Catherine de Medici, withdrew his support from the humanists, who were associated with Lutheranism. In October 1534, the crisis came. Certain radical Protestants plastered posters on the same night all over Paris, Orleans, Rouen and other cities, denouncing the Mass in extreme language. One poster was even put on the King's own chamber. Francis I was enraged, and Protestants were hunted down mercilessly. Calvin only escaped by leaving his possessions and income and fleeing under a false name. In 1536, a refugee in Basel, he published the first edition of *Institutes of the Christian Religion*.

The book made Calvin famous as a Protestant. While travelling in June 1536, he stopped overnight in Geneva. When the Genevan Reformer Guillaume

Farel heard that Calvin was in town, he went immediately to his rooms and begged the Frenchman to stay. Calvin did not particularly want to, but Farel insisted that this was the work of God and must not be denied. Calvin came to agree; and for the rest of his life Geneva became his primary ministry.

The work Calvin undertook in Geneva was very different from the scholarly life he had led before, even in exile. At Geneva he was a pastor and statesman, learning how to organize a church and continue the reformation begun by the city council. Biblical principles now had to be transformed into practical ideas for living, and many of the citizens resisted changes to the old lifestyle with its medieval religion. Calvin disliked controversy and politics intensely. He would have preferred to remain a scholar. Nevertheless, he took on this job with the same self-discipline and determination that he had shown in his scholarly work, reminding himself of his conviction that he was doing God's work.

Calvin and Farel did not have positions of authority in Geneva. Calvin was not even invited to become a citizen until he had been there twenty years, and that was only eight years before he died. Nonetheless, between them, Calvin and Farel made Geneva a Protestant city, which meant moral as well as doctrinal reformation. In a city that had a name for gambling and drunkenness, and the moral corruption of its leaders, many citizens resisted.

Unfortunately, the city council and the Reformers could not agree over who should have the final say in matters of church discipline, especially excommunication. Because of this, Calvin and Farel were exiled by the city council. Calvin went to Strasbourg, and returned to his academic lifestyle, teaching and preaching to French exiles. In 1541, Geneva called him back; the city had reached new heights of confusion, and leading councillors recognized a need for the reforming guidance offered by Calvin. Calvin apparently left Strasbourg in tears; he did not want to go back to the anxious lifestyle of a pastor of a reluctant church. Nonetheless, his iron will took him back to what he still considered to be God's work.

Calvin married in 1540—not quite the misogynist of the modern 'Calvin legend'. What did horrify him, however, was the sexual license of many of the upper-class women of the city, who vigorously opposed his efforts at moral reform. In fact, throughout all the classes of the city, Calvin was appalled at the moral laxity. His new Church Ordinance was accepted, but the struggle to implement his suggested changes took time. His idea for church order included enforcing moral discipline through a court of ministers and elders. In time, the ministers of this church court would take over the social and moral discipline of the city.

Despite Calvin's intentions, a court of this nature was open to misuse. It was too easily used as an opportunity to humiliate people in public. As Calvin continued to press his reforms on all classes uniformly, resistance increased. As long as he agreed with the council to close houses of prostitution and tried to reduce drunkenness, the civil authorities had not protested. When equally stringent rules began to be applied to the behaviour of the upper class, they became increasingly hostile. Calvin's life can never have been pleasant, as he personally hated the battles that his own convictions were bringing upon him.

In 1553, the death of the heretic Michael Servetus provided a climax for the clash between Calvin and his council opponents. Servetus had already attacked Calvin in print, denying the doctrine of the Trinity, among other issues. He had already been arrested once in Geneva and escaped. Why he chose to come back to Geneva is hard to understand, but when Calvin was made aware of his presence, Servetus was arrested again. He was tried for heresy and sentenced to burning.

Calvin's reputation has suffered ever since then because of this incident. Servetus was indeed a violent heretic, and the Roman Catholic church was also seeking him vigorously. The city council captured, tried and executed Servetus. Calvin was called as an expert witness; he was not the prosecutor. Calvin tried to have the death-sentence reduced to the more merciful means of execution by beheading. Apart from the cruelty of a death by burning, Calvin supported the council. Along with the rest of the church, both medieval and reformed, Calvin believed that Servetus' heresy was so bad that it amounted to the murder of the souls seduced by it.

It is somewhat ironic that this episode, which has since so tarnished Calvin's reputation, at the time led to his triumph in Geneva. Calvin's main opponents on the council had supported Servetus, and his condemnation as a heretic destroyed their position. In 1555, several agitators on the council left, and Calvin was finally left with a sympathetic council.

Under Calvin, the disciplinary procedures of the church fulfilled the council's desire to reform the city. Laws were passed against blasphemy and adultery, and to enforce church attendance; also Calvin urged that schooling be made compulsory, as well as laws concerning public health. The level of public devotion to God and godliness should not be looked upon too sceptically. The city was not hypocritical under Calvin; dissenters were free to leave, and if the enforcement of godly behaviour was grumbled against, it was not the anger of rebellion. Calvin was determined that the truth would provide the best way to live.

Overall, the Swiss Reformation was characterized by an emphasis on discipline and reform of manners, not just theology and church practice. Social issues such as welfare policy and schooling benefited. One of the most important features of the Swiss Reformation was that it was, like that of the other city-states of southern Germany, a lay reformation. It was a reform of society as well as a reform of church.

This was most successful in French-speaking Switzerland. After the suppression of the Peasants' War, common people in German-speaking Switzerland withdrew much of their support from the Reformation. Reformers and secular authorities, in response to the excesses of the peasants, made it clear that religious reform was not necessarily linked with social reform. It was at this stage that Anabaptism veered off into a different reforming path, partly because of disillusionment with Zwingli's reform. The Swiss Brethren separated from the established church and soon after were harshly suppressed, especially by the city councils of Zurich and Berne.

3 France

The Reformation made a beginning in France, but eventually was crushed by the hostility of the monarch. Unlike the German princes, the French King was not inclined to challenge the church. To do so would have cost him far more than it would have gained. The monarchy in France was considered something religious in itself; the king was believed to be God's elect, with mystical powers such as the healing of the disease scrofula. Kings promised on coronation to expel all heretics, and to go back on that promise would seem to be a denial of God and the throne. It would take a rash monarch to challenge the church.

Also in France, as in other places, cardinals were very powerful. This was necessary for the country to function. The king of France was ruler of a vast territory, one that threatened to splinter if he challenged the other leading authority in the land. Religion and the monarchy were the only things that held France together; there was no common language, no national identity, no unity of legal customs or history. Many areas of France had only been brought into the kingdom in the previous century. The monarchy simply could not afford to be sympathetic to change. Even if the king had wanted change, he would have had a hard time fighting his senior officials, who more often than not bought their offices—meaning they could not be fired.

Although initially the Protestant message had spread through France, and many communities formed around Protestant principles, persecution was not long in following. From around 1543, organized dispersal of Protestant communities began. However, at the start it was not the King who began repression of the Reformation, but senior magistrates and various factions loyal to Rome. They did not bother waiting for the King's permission; indeed, some of the early decisions to round up Protestants and destroy their bookshops were made when the King was not even in the country.

At first the persecution did not work; the more trials there were, the more heretics there seemed to be. Paradoxically, under this persecution the Reformation spread, and in 1559 there was even a First National Synod of Protestants. Orthodox Catholics began to panic. The French Reformation was by now strongly influenced by Calvin, and congregations looked to Geneva to appoint their ministers and to settle disputes. Calvin encouraged civil obedience, and made this clear in repeated public statements, even letters addressed to the King. It was not enough; Protestantism was still extremely threatening to the monarchy.

There was a brief glimmer of hope in the early 1550s. King Henry II was in dispute with the papacy over a number of issues, and began strengthening his alliances with the German Protestant princes. It looked as if some sympathy for the Protestants might be forthcoming. However, the power structure of France prevented Henry from following his own policies. His cardinals acted against him, and Henry turned again to persecuting Protestants. Calvin gave up hope for support from the French monarchy.

Nonetheless, the gospel continued to do its work, and the years 1561-2 were the peak of French Protestantism. This was aided by a sudden weakening of the central power. Factionalism and bankruptcy had unexpectedly struck at the monarchy and, more importantly, at the very machinery of prosecution

The Massacre of St Bartholomew

for heresy. Calvin was overwhelmed with requests
for pastors. The Protestants even had hope of a new
supportive monarchy in 1560, when Charles IX came
to the throne as a child. His oldest relative, Antoine
de Bourbon, was the natural choice for regent and he
would most likely have supported the Huguenots, the
French evangelical party. Unfortunately, undecided

about what he should do, he delayed too long. The King's mother, the staunchly traditional Catherine de Medici, declared herself regent.

It was as a result of Catherine's influence that the infamous Massacre of St Bartholomew took place. This was a ruthless, planned killing of known groups of Protestants in Autumn 1572. Contemporaries portrayed it as loyal citizens destroying enemies who planned to kill the King. However, Protestants insisted that they had always been loyal to the monarchy and were betrayed. Catherine de Medici and other royal councillors hated them. It was clear that Protestants could not trust the monarchy ever again.

In 1589-1593, France had a Protestant monarch, Henry IV, but he stood to lose half his kingdom, as the rest refused to serve a heretic king. He tried to win them by force, but failed. He changed sides—rejected his Protestant faith and insisted he was Catholic—in 1593. France has had only a minimal Protestant population ever since.

4 Scotland

Scotland probably demonstrated the most thorough reformation of any country. In contrast to other countries, there was very little loss of life or civil unrest as the Reformation was carried through. Contempt for the morals of the clergy was widespread, and ideas from the various pre-Reformation heretical movements (such as the Hussites) were widely present in Scotland, if not openly proclaimed.

Resistance slowly stirred against the medieval orthodoxy during the first few decades of the sixteenth century, and it was only increased by a growing persecution of those who possessed New Testaments or seemed to hold to Reformed doctrines. Some were burned at the stake or punished in other ways, and several fled. However, the clergy were clearly losing control. Popular satires held up clergy lifestyles to ridicule all over the country. The persecutions did very little to quell the rising anti-church sentiment, and probably only encouraged it.

The Reformation proper in Scotland was led by John Knox. He had lived an adventurous life: he had fought the French, and spent nineteen months as a French slave, before escaping to England. At this time, Edward VI was on the throne and the English Reformation was well under way. Knox became one of the King's preachers, and spent his time with the most dedicated of the English Reformers. Like them, his life was put in danger when Edward died and Mary came to the throne. He fled to Europe to stay with Calvin in Geneva.

In 1559, Knox returned to Scotland. With his first sermon in St Andrews Castle, he began to focus the general feelings of resentment against the church into a Protestant movement. The main danger was external. France and Spain were by this

John Knox

time fiercely anti-Protestant, and there was a real fear that the French fleet would attack Scotland to enforce a return to the medieval church. Scotland had a history of strong ties with France; Mary Guise, Queen of Scotland, was at the time living in France, married to the dauphin (crown prince). There were French troops garrisoned in Scotland, and Scotland was strategically important to France as a base for attacking England. As alliance with Protestantism effectively meant enmity to France, the French were considerably disturbed by the Scottish Reformation.

Unlikely elements were used by God to protect the Scottish Reformers in this political tangle. Queen

Elizabeth's advisers, seeing the threat to England if France regained control of Scotland, persuaded her to an alliance with the Protestants of Scotland. She finally agreed, and in an historically unprecedented event, a friendly English force entered Edinburgh in 1560. At the same time, France was shaken by a sudden bankruptcy, and Protestantism there was at its height. Distracted by internal problems, France did not arrange any attack on Scotland.

Knox and his associates drew up a statement of Reformed doctrine, which was accepted by the Scottish parliament. There were still to be threats to this religious peace, as Mary Queen of Scots who returned to Scotland in 1561 was staunchly Catholic, and her heir, the young James VI, shifted alliances for his own ends. (It is ironic that it was his name that was attached to the translation of the Bible that was central to Protestant Christianity for so long.) Nevertheless, during Knox's lifetime and after, Scotland remained determinedly Protestant.

5 England

The Reformation in England began slowly, as the shocking news of Luther's rebellion reached England. In the early sixteenth century, England was staunchly Roman. Henry VIII had come to the throne in 1509, a popular and vigorous young king, who seemed to promise prosperity and good fortune for England. He was a devout young man who had at one stage thought of entering the priesthood. Indeed, he had studied theology before his elder brother Arthur died, making Henry the heir to the throne. Henry, a loyal son of the church, strictly opposed Luther and received the title (still held by the English monarch) 'Defender of the faith' for his treatise *On the Seven Sacraments*, refuting Luther's theology.

As Lutheran ideas began to seep into the country, one particular place to find them was Cambridge. Here, academics and students from the university would meet at one of the local taverns to discuss Luther's ideas, and read the New Testament in Greek. This interest in the new theology had been given encouragement by Erasmus, the Dutch humanist scholar who had criticized church practices and had published the New Testament in Greek. Erasmus' purpose had in fact been to purify the Latin Bible. His edition contained the old, Vulgate Latin translation and his new translation, and the Greek was merely included as extra material to prove that his Latin was better than the old. Erasmus was not a Protestant; he wanted the church to be rid of its corruption and superstitions, but he had no wish to change the basic theology. When he visited Cambridge, he gave lectures describing his views. The effect of his visit, however, was to stimulate new interest in the Greek text of the Bible, and some of the scholars there began to look at their theology from a new perspective.

William Tyndale

a) Tyndale

One of those possibly at these discussions was William Tyndale. Tyndale was never a church official in England, but exerted a foundational influence on the English Reformation because of his translation of the New Testament into English and his writings on behalf of Reformation doctrine. The translation of Scripture into the common language was essential to the genuinely religious part of the Reformation, which arose not from politics, or desire for social reform, but from the discovery of the word of God. It gave ordinary people the means to know God's message directly, without the mediation of the church, or indeed censorship of the church. Before Tyndale, there were various English-language paraphrases of the life of Christ, and homilies for devotional use, but none of these explained the essential content of the New Testament. Unauthorized translation of the Bible into English was illegal.

Nonetheless, the English people had a tradition of reading the Bible in secret; in the previous century, John Wycliffe had produced a (rather bad) English translation, which circulated in manuscript. Anyone owning it, or professing Wycliffe's theology, was fiercely persecuted. This movement (the Lollard movement) had, however, generated an undercurrent of early 'Protestant' thought, which anticipated the popularity of Tyndale's Bible.

In 1522, Tyndale took up a position as tutor in a Gloucestershire house, with ample time for preaching at the surrounding villages and in Bristol. Dismayed by the theology and lack of biblical knowledge of the clergy he found, Tyndale decided to translate the New Testament into English. He moved to London and sought an interview with Bishop Tunstall to ask for support for this project, which was denied. Tyndale continued in London, preaching Reformation doctrine, until in 1524 he sailed for Hamburg, realizing he would be unable to accomplish the translation while in England.

On the continent, Tyndale spent some time with Luther while completing his translation, which he arranged to have published in Cologne. The work was interrupted, so Tyndale moved to Worms and there he finished the publication. Copies of the English New Testament were smuggled into England, and by 1526 it had been denounced and banned by the Bishop of London. This was surprising: Bishop Tunstall was a fine Greek scholar who would have been able to tell (better than most) that Tyndale's translation was accurate. Neither were there any marginal notes, or commentary, that could have been taken as preaching heretical doctrine. The published New Testament was simply the text translated into English.

The books continued to be distributed secretly, and Cardinal Wolsey tried to have Tyndale seized at Worms; but Tyndale escaped to Marburg. During the next few years Tyndale published strongly Protestant writings that were distributed in England. He also began Old Testament translation, though was handicapped by losing all his papers in a shipwreck in 1529. He proceeded to Hamburg and continued to write forcefully against the Roman church. At this time, Tyndale also entered his literary debate with Sir Thomas More, who had been invited by Tunstall to defend the church against the new heresies. In 1531, Henry VIII demanded Tyndale's surrender from the Emperor Charles V on the charge of spreading sedition in England. Charles was unsympathetic to Henry (being the nephew of one of Henry's rejected wives, Catherine of Aragon) and Tyndale was kept safe.

However, Tyndale was in a dangerous position. He was living in the house of Thomas Pointz, an English merchant. This was in Antwerp, a town that was quite friendly to Reformation doctrines, and while he was there he was reasonably secure. He had the freedom and the resources to continue his translation work. Nonetheless, Charles V was still ruler and still considered Reformation doctrines heresy, and his court was only twenty-four miles away. As long as Tyndale stayed with an influential Englishman, whose trading brought considerable profit to the town, it was unlikely he would be arrested.

It was a fellow Englishman who was Tyndale's downfall. Henry Phillips, a gentleman's son, had fallen into disgrace with his family through theft and gambling. How he turned to secret dealings is not known, but it is evident that someone in London paid him well to capture Tyndale. He travelled to Louvain, still staunchly Roman, and sought refuge, claiming (probably truthfully) that he was totally against King Henry and Lutheranism. From there he carried out his plot to arrest Tyndale. As an Englishman, it was fairly easy to meet Tyndale in the company of English merchants. Tyndale, apparently unsuspecting, befriended him. Although Tyndale's host Pointz was suspicious, he spent some part of his time travelling and was away one evening when Phillips came to visit Tyndale. He invited Tyndale out for dinner; Tyndale came, and fell into the hands of the officers from Charles' court whom Phillips had waiting.

Tyndale was tried for heresy on the continent in 1536 and was executed in October of that year, strangled first then burned. Phillips saw his arrest through to the end; at one point, when it seemed that Pointz was going to be able to bring sufficient pressure to bear to have Tyndale released, Phillips had Pointz accused of heresy and imprisoned. It is still not known who was behind the plot to kill Tyndale; most likely not King Henry. Phillips disappeared into obscurity soon afterwards.

b) Henry and Cranmer

Meanwhile, Henry VIII had been experiencing his own problems. He had been married to Catherine of Aragon for going on seventeen years, but was still without an heir. The only one of Catherine's children to survive had been their daughter Mary. Henry, not to mention the rest of England, had no wish to risk a controversy over who would be heir to the throne. He was keen to marry a young lady he had recently met—the (Protestant) Anne Boleyn. Henry applied for an annulment of his first marriage. To his surprise, the papal court hesitated, and despite tedious negotiation, by 1529 had still failed to make a decision. Henry was getting impatient.

There were, after all, grounds for Henry to ask for

the divorce. Catherine had been married to Henry's brother, Arthur, who had died before becoming king. As the new heir, Henry had married her; her considerable dowry no doubt provided incentive. However, this was not legal by Canon law, and Pope Julius II had been asked to grant a dispensation to make the marriage possible.

Because the marriage was without an heir, however, Henry was able to suggest that this was the judgement of God for marrying his brother's widow. He argued that the marriage was never lawful, so he should be granted a divorce. Such divorces were not unusual, and Henry expected no setback. Pope Clement VII, however, was in a difficult position. First of all, to grant the divorce he would have to rescind a dispensation given by a previous pope. Such an action was difficult for an institution that was supposed to be conservative and stable. What is more, this was 1529; and in 1527 Emperor Charles V had invaded Italy and now had the Pope under his power. Charles V, by one of those coincidences not unusual among a small ruling elite, was Catherine of Aragon's nephew. Pope Clement would hardly have wished to antagonize Charles by declaring his aunt a whore—as she would be, if the marriage was declared illegal from the start.

Henry began to take political action against the ecclesiastical administration. In 1529, a young theologian, Thomas Cranmer, had left Cambridge

Thomas Cranmer

because of pestilence there and moved with two other scholars to their father's house at Waltham Abbey. Here, at the same house, two of Henry VIII's chief agents in his divorce also lodged for a while. In conversation Cranmer gave his opinion that Henry should consult divines at his own English universities as to the validity of his first marriage, rather than pursue his cause at Rome. Cranmer's opinion was reported to the King who, greatly pleased, summoned Cranmer and appointed him to write a treatise and dispute the matter at Cambridge. The Cambridge divines concurred with Cranmer's view of the invalidity of the first marriage.

In 1531, Henry took an astonishing step. He charged the whole of the English clergy with treason for accepting the authority of Wolsey, the papal legate in England. He used the statute of Praemunire, an old law to safeguard against excessive foreign influence in England, but which was certainly never meant for Henry's purpose. With supreme irony, Henry condemned his clergy for obeying the church authority that they not only vowed to obey on their ordination, but to which he had so far been loyal! To be restored, Henry charged them £118000, and insisted that they recognize him as the supreme head of the church in England.

Legally, the battle was over in 1532 when the clergy submitted their canon-making power to the king. In 1533, Henry secretly married Anne Boleyn, considering himself no longer bound to wait for papal sanction. He continued with his legal changes; in that same year, the Act for Restraint of Appeals was passed, which stopped all appeals to Rome, so any spiritual matters must now be decided in the king's courts.

Cranmer had accompanied Henry's ambassador to a meeting of the Pope and Emperor Charles V at Bologna in 1530. He was thereafter sent on various diplomatic missions until recalled to England in 1532 to become Archbishop of Canterbury. This promotion came as a surprise for him—a particular difficulty was that he had married in Germany, and how to look after his wife in secret remained a problem for many years. However, the summons was authoritative, and in 1533 Cranmer arrived in England (having sent his wife before him) and took up the archbishopric with the disclaimer that his obedience to the Pope would not come before his loyalty to the King or prevent him from reforming anything he found amiss in England. On 23 May of that year, Cranmer pronounced Catherine's marriage invalid and five days later pronounced the King lawfully married to Anne Boleyn. The Archbishop now had considerable power as the highest ecclesiastical authority recognized in England, and set about annoying his clergy with visitations.

Henry was not an easy master to serve. In 1535, Sir Thomas More and Bishop Fisher, two prominent members of the church, were beheaded for refusing to swear to the royal supremacy (Cranmer apparently tried to prevent their execution). People were shocked at Henry's brutality against these men, known for their piety. At this stage, the reformation was entirely Henry's; the country was still theologically medieval, just not under Rome's authority. Henry, growing increasingly bad-tempered (he still did not have an heir), seemed to be mainly interested in his own power. Any dissenters, regardless of their theology, were his enemies.

Around this time the 'visitation of the monasteries' began, which led to their dissolution. That is, the monks were thrown out, the monasteries and their lands seized for the King, and any treasures removed. This process was overseen by Thomas Cromwell (great-great-uncle of Oliver Cromwell, who was to cause such a stir in the next century). While abuses and immorality among the monks were given as reasons, it is likely that Cromwell's zeal sprang mostly from the money to be made by seizing church lands.

In 1536, Anne Boleyn was executed, accused of witchcraft. She had failed to give Henry a son; her only child was Elizabeth. Henry had discarded one wife and killed another for their failure to produce heirs, even though both their daughters were to become queens of England.

However, Anne Boleyn seems to have had some influence on Henry, as had his now strongly Protestant Archbishop Thomas Cranmer. Later in 1536, an Act was passed that affected the theology of the church, not just its political structure. The Act of Ten Articles, largely produced by Cranmer, contained Lutheran ideas. The split with Rome was beginning to be a reformation, not just a schism. In 1537, Cranmer requested that the sale of Matthew's Bible, based on Tyndale's translation, be authorized, and in 1540 ordered that this Bible be placed in every church in England.

Nonetheless, Henry was still a dubious ally for

the Reformers. By 1539, the Act of Ten Articles had been countered by the Act of Six Articles, a return to traditional doctrine. Henry also had another reason for rejoicing; he finally had his heir. He had married Jane Seymour in 1536, and within a year she had produced Henry's first son, Edward. Jane Seymour died in the same year.

During all this, Cranmer was on shaky ground, trying to mitigate Henry's treatment of his fourth and fifth wives, as well as holding a contentious doctrinal position. Cranmer survived several conspiracies against him, defended by Henry, who appeared to be fond enough of his archbishop to overlook theological differences not tolerated in other men.

The rest of Henry's life was marked mainly by his atrocious attitude to his wives, and his increasing severity on any dissidents who happened to displease him. In 1540, Henry had married and divorced Anne of Cleves and married Katharine Howard. Two years later Katherine Howard was beheaded on a charge of adultery, and Henry married his sixth wife, Katharine Parr. Henry finally died in 1547.

c) The Reformation consolidated

This was a new opportunity for England, and for those who wanted to see the church genuinely reformed. Edward VI was still a child, but old enough to agree that he preferred Protestant doctrines to traditional ones. Cranmer had been named in Henry's will as one of the council to govern during Edward's minority. Cranmer appears to have advocated a more conservative policy in religious change at first, but soon dramatic alterations began to take place. In 1548, a royal commission was appointed to revise the offices of the church; this commission consisted of six bishops and six other divines, presided over by Cranmer. It is generally recognized that most of the wording of the new Prayer Book of 1549 was Cranmer's, as was that of the revised book of 1552. He also translated many of the Collects from the medieval Latin order, and these translations have been praised as masterpieces of English prose.

However, the religious innovations were causing widespread dissension. In 1549, a serious insurrection in Devonshire and Cornwall took place, the rebels demanding the restoration of the old religion. There was increasing political tension at court between the conservative and Reforming parties. Due to various political machinations, Edward's protector, the Duke of Somerset, was executed in 1552 and the more ruthless Northumberland took up the position. (It was Northumberland who engineered the plot to pronounce Lady Jane Grey queen on Edward's death.)

In 1553, Edward, always a weak child, died. His older sister, daughter of Catherine of Aragon, became Queen Mary. Mary, like her mother, was fiercely Roman Catholic and just as determined to see what she considered to be the true church reinstated. It was bad news for the Reformers. Several key church-men were able to escape to Europe, to spend time with Calvin or in Lutheran Germany; many others did not escape. Thomas Cranmer, and some of his key bishops, were burned at the stake for heresy. Over three hundred people were killed for heresy during Mary's five-year reign.

The country was in a state of considerable tension when Mary died in 1558. Her sister, Anne Boleyn's daughter Elizabeth, was crowned Elizabeth I; but was she going to make England Protestant? In an effort to gain some peace for the country, Elizabeth returned to the Protestant church, with a popular following reacting against the deaths under Mary. It was not the church that the most radical of the Reformers had envisaged; Elizabeth was too clever a politician to let the radicals have their way. Nonetheless, it was a Protestant church, and one to which the Reformers who had escaped from Mary could return—the beginnings of the Puritan Party.

Part III

A new world

1 Did doctrine matter?

Why don't you cry out against bad popes rather than against all popes?

Erasmus to Luther, 1519

One way of understanding the difference that the Reformation made is to compare the Reformation program with that of another 'reformer' who wanted to purify the medieval church: Erasmus of Rotterdam. He was a man who was just as much against moral corruption, injustice and superstition as any of the Reformers. He was just as passionate and just as eager for the church to change. However, in his basic view of how to relate to God, he remained loyal to medieval theology. This highlights for us the crucial differences between the medieval world and the Reformation world. It was much more than just reaction against corruption. It was a change in fundamental beliefs about God, humanity and the world.

For decades before Luther's revolt, people had wanted church reform. The general intellectual movement known as the Renaissance affected theology as well as philosophy. Because of this movement, as well as frustration at the financial and moral corruption of the church, some people began to speak out. Erasmus of Rotterdam was one of the most outspoken of these critics. He was a scholar of the Low Country who began his career in monastic circumstances, though he later professed a dislike for the religious orders. Erasmus was an eloquent and humorous writer and was famous throughout Europe as a learned scholar and wise critic of the Roman church. His works included an edition of the New Testament in Greek, as well as a new critical edition of Jerome's Latin Bible and paraphrases of the New Testament.

Erasmus commented on weaknesses in state and church in a satire, *The Praise of Folly* (first published 1511). His criticisms sounded very similar to those the Reformers were to make. He wrote of the fools who "delight in miracles and fictitious marvels, whether hearing or telling about them"—people who relied upon the healing or protective powers of saints and their images. He derided faith in the bones of saints, the set chants, and the ceremonial devotion. Just as silly in Erasmus' eyes were the local loyalties to particular saints, attributing the relief of particular ills to each one. This "sea of superstition" pervaded the lives of ordinary Christians everywhere and were encouraged by the priests who were "not unaware of the profit to be made thereby".

Another example of religious folly, according to Erasmus, was that people believed certain prayers or deeds could reduce the time to be spent in purgatory—as if there were some mathematical table by which to calculate the exact number of months or hours there that were due to a person. Monks and monasteries also received his sarcasm. After poking fun at the rigidity of the rules, and their delight in ignorance and dirtiness, Erasmus claimed that monks were more interested in keeping their own ceremonies than God's commands.

Here we begin to see where Erasmus' reforms were different from the Reformers' reforms. Religious activities are well and good, Erasmus wrote, if they are really done for the end of greater godliness and service of Christ. For instance, a person should fast, not simply to abstain from food as an end in itself, nor to appear pious, but as an exercise to quell the passions and be more godly. If a person eats, it should be to remain strong enough for devotional pursuits and prayerful vigils, not to stay good-looking. The end must always be greater godliness or the activity is useless. Similarly, there was no problem with the worship of saints, but the selfishness with which it was done reduced it to the level of pagan religion.

True worship of any saint, he claimed, was to copy their virtues. If you wish to honour St Francis, then, like him, be humble and despise riches. If you wish to worship Christ through his saints, well and good, but "see to it that you imitate Christ in the saints", do not just go through the outward observances. Holiness or spirituality exist in moral activities, not in rituals or ceremonies performed; and the rituals properly understood are only aids to these spiritual qualities.

In the issue of ceremony, prayer and saints, then, Erasmus presented views and criticisms very similar to those of the Reformers. He insisted that God was to be worshipped by an inward change of heart, not by ceremonies; that prayer was a genuine inner plea, and did not work better because of the length or number of prayers chanted; and that the saints were to be copied, not given gifts as the pagans did their gods. Yet there were radical differences between the nature of the criticisms Erasmus made and those made by the Reformers. In Erasmus' view, for instance, a saint had the power to dispense favours—Erasmus merely derided the greedy use of this power. In the same way, Erasmus criticized the misuse or over-emphasis of the value of ceremonies; but he still thought them a correct way to approach God. His alternative to an 'outward' religion was not the Protestant 'faith alone' but 'faith plus charity'.

The doctrinal battle that Erasmus was finally pushed to having with Luther was on free will, and illustrates the basic divide between his ideas and the theology of the Reformation. The issue was whether man was capable of fulfilling the demands of God. Luther claimed that it was not possible—that the commands in Scripture to perfect behaviour only highlighted man's imperfection and inability to live up to the standard. Recognizing his helplessness, man can only cease to rely on himself and throw himself wholly on God's mercy. This doctrine is justification by faith alone, in which a person is declared just or right before God *only* through trusting in Christ. Erasmus agreed that salvation is by faith alone, but argued that man's deeds do contribute something—that man can in a sense cooperate with God in salvation; to which Luther replied that it was therefore no longer by faith *alone*. It was a contrast between a view in which man was only and utterly dependent on God, and one in which man could actively cooperate in his path to heaven.

In fact, Erasmus was truly a reformer, in the sense that he wanted to purify the church as it was. The Reformers were actually revolutionaries, overthrowing the old views for something radically different. Erasmus was not a Protestant; he was an exceptionally good Catholic. He wished to strengthen the church, and bring it to a purer holiness as he perceived it. The Reformers rejected the medieval church as part of a wrong understanding of the world, and preached a new one. Erasmus was not essentially a precursor to the Reformation; he lived in a different world, the world that the Reformers rejected.

What was this new world of belief that the Reformers preached? And how did it relate to the practices of medieval Catholicism that they were criticizing?

2 The doctrinal issues

a) The slogans

One of the clearest summaries of the doctrinal issues that were at stake in the Reformation is the slogan coined by Martin Luther to describe his position: *sola gratia* (by grace alone), *sola Christi* (by Christ alone), *sola Scriptura* (by Scripture alone), *sola fide* (by faith alone). In essence, these Latin phrases were Luther's answer to four basic questions:

How can a person be right with God? *Sola gratia* (by grace alone). The only way that sinful human beings can come back into a right relationship with God is through God's initiative alone. It is not because some of us are more deserving, or have earned his favour. God freely and graciously saves those who cannot save themselves. It is all from God.

How does this grace come? *Sola Christi* (by Christ alone). God chooses to be gracious to us in a particular way, through a particular channel—through Jesus Christ. His generosity and kindness to us is mediated not through priests or rituals or religion or anything else, but through Christ alone, and in particular through his death and resurrection.

How do we find Christ? *Sola Scriptura* (through Scripture alone). Against those who would say that Christ is to be found through mystical experience, or through the authoritative teaching of the church, Luther argued that Scripture alone is the one, true place where Christ's voice is heard.

What is our part? *Sola fide* (by faith alone). Our response to God's grace in Christ that is found in Scripture is faith—that is, a personal trust in God, that what he has promised to do for us in Christ he will do. This glad trust in God then results in a changed way of living. Luther put it like this: "Faith is a living and unshakeable confidence, a belief in the grace of God so assured that a man would die a thousand deaths for its sake. This kind of confidence in God's grace, this sort of knowledge of it, makes us joyful, high-spirited, and eager in our relations with God and with all mankind. This is what the Holy Spirit effects through faith. Hence the man of faith, without being driven, willingly and gladly seeks to do good to everyone, serve everyone, suffer all kinds of hardships, for the sake of the love and the glory of the God who has shown him such grace."

These four foundational doctrines of the Reformation, which we have summarized only briefly, had enormous implications. It was because of these beliefs that the Reformers knew they could no longer remain within the Roman Catholic church. Unlike Erasmus, they were not content merely to call the church back to be more faithful to its existing doctrine. The Reformers were convinced that the Roman church had departed from biblical Christianity at these crucial points.

Let us look at some of the particular areas in

which these Reformation doctrines collided with the practice of Roman Catholicism.

b) The Mass

The Reformation belief that God's grace came to people by Christ alone, and was grasped in response by faith alone, had immediate implications for the sacraments. As we saw in Part I, the sacraments—and in particular the Mass—were a central part of medieval Catholicism. In the Mass, the actual body of Christ was present (by transubstantiation) and was offered up by the priest as a sacrifice for the sins of the people—a kind of re-enactment of the crucifixion. By eating the body of Christ thus sacrificed, the believer was able to receive God's grace.

The Reformers rejected the doctrine of the Mass as unbiblical. The saving power of the death and resurrection of Jesus Christ, in their view, was entirely the work of God and not mankind. The benefits could only be received by faith or trust in the God who had made such benefits possible. For humans to take on God's role in a re-sacrifice was not only ridiculous, but also blasphemous.

Moreover, the Mass was part of a whole sacramental system whereby God's grace was mediated to the individual through signs and rituals and priests, rather than God's grace coming only through Christ.

It was for this issue—the rejection of transubstantiation and the Mass—that most of the martyrs of the

Reformation died. Both sides saw that to deny the doctrine of the Mass was more than a slight difference of opinion or a call for superficial reform; it struck at the heart of medieval Catholicism and its sacramental theology.

The general consensus among the Reformers was that Jesus had only commanded two sacraments, the Lord's Supper and baptism. Essentially, they defined 'sacraments' in terms of promise. They were actions or symbols that in some way expressed or reminded people of a promise of God concerning salvation. So the sacrament was entirely bound up with God's ability to keep his promises. There was no power in the object of the sacrament itself, apart from its calling forth the response of faith and trust in God. Thus the Lord's Supper was a testimony to Jesus' death, which brought salvation, and baptism a preaching of the renewal by the Holy Spirit in regeneration. The five other traditional sacraments were generally regarded as good and proper things to do, providing they were correctly understood. However, they should not be made obligatory as part of church life.

Opinions on the Lord's Supper itself varied between Reformers. Luther, the first to make the distinctive doctrinal break on this matter, denounced *transubstantiation* as unbiblical and untrue. Nonetheless, Luther still held that the body of Christ was really present in the bread, in a mysterious way. It was Zwingli in Switzerland who pushed this further, insisting that the bread and wine remain simply bread and wine, and function as a symbol or reminder of the gospel that Christ died for us. The ceremony of the Lord's Supper, according to Zwingli, is a public testimony to the faith of Christians. Calvin in Geneva had a slightly different view again, closer to Zwingli's than Luther's, which is also broadly speaking where the Reformers of England and Scotland took their stand.

c) The Pope and the word of God

The medieval church did not accept the Bible as the sole authority for knowledge of God. It was believed that doctrine could also come from elsewhere— from tradition, as the church developed ideas and important theologians discussed them. Certain 'unwritten truths' were accepted as authoritative, as passed down through the church even though they were not found in the Bible. Scripture itself had to be interpreted according to the official teachings of the church—which contained scriptural and unscriptural elements. Students studying theology at university were not allowed to study the Bible until they had years of studying ancient philosophers and church tradition. The Bible was seen as a book with many layers of interpretation, not one that could simply be read on its own.

The Reformers, on the other hand, insisted on 'Scripture alone'. Christ came to his people and ruled them and spoke to them not through the church, but through the Bible. The place of the church was to sit under Christ's authority—that is, to sit under the Scriptures, and obey the Scriptures, not become an equal authority and in practice subvert the Scriptures. It was impossible, said the Reformers, for the church to produce extra-biblical authoritative doctrine, for all the promises of God found their yes and amen in Jesus Christ (2 Cor 1:20). Nothing ought to be added to Scripture, for such is the rebelliousness of the human mind with respect to knowledge of God, that any attempt to find knowledge of God outside "Christ clothed with the gospel" (as Luther put it) was doomed to be misleading and futile. In this way they rejected the idea of an evolving theology, in which tradition could be added to Scripture. The Scriptures were both sufficient and necessary and nothing more ought to be said. The proper role of the church was to confess the teaching of Scripture.

The next battle was to demand that Scripture be available to everyone. It should not be kept from people, either by prohibition or by lack of availability through being in a foreign tongue (i.e. ancient Greek or Latin). Scripture, because it is the word of God, was held to be the means to life itself, and something that *must* be available in the common language. It was ridiculous to argue that ordinary people were not worthy to study Scripture, for it was God's communication to all mankind, not merely to an elite.

Henry VIII being presented with a
copy of the Bible in English

The fact that the Bible was translated into common languages—into German by Luther, and into English by Tyndale—had a dramatic effect on the progress of the Reformation. Quite apart from the knowledge it gave people, this act symbolized a totally different attitude to relationship with God. It put into the hands of ordinary people the means to listen to the voice of Christ, and therefore to reject any teaching that was contrary to it, even if it was a teaching put forward by the church authorities. Reformers denied that uneducated people could not understand what was in Scripture. This insulted God's ability to communicate to his people.

We can understand, then, the sheer exasperation that the Reformers showed with people who wished to continue church services in Latin. Cranmer's harassed tone emerges in his letter to the rebels of Devon, when they demanded a return to Latin: "But I would gladly know the reason why the Cornish men refuse utterly the new English, as you call it, because certain of you understand it not; and yet you will have the service in Latin, which almost none of you understand". Understanding the Word was all-important, for without an understanding of that, ceremonial actions were meaningless, and therefore useless. What is more, any exposition of Scripture must do justice to the text; there could be no extracting of 'proof-texts', taken out of context, or having an improbable interpretation placed upon them. Any exposition had to be supported by textual evidence. The text itself must be allowed to speak, or rather the Author behind the text.

To be Christian meant that one had the Holy Spirit, who would enlighten the mind to understand Scripture. By emphasizing this, the Reformers asserted that Scripture was God's very words, spoken by his breath, the Spirit. This doctrine redefined what it meant to be in contact with God. Such contact meant understanding a message that would have a life-changing effect as the hearer was obedient to what God said.

d) Saints and images
Most leaders of the Reformation forbade saint-worship outright, and many shrines were destroyed.

It was regarded as idolatry, the worship of false gods. In England, specific instructions were given for the dismantling of the apparatus of saint worship. Clergy were disciplined if they encouraged veneration of saints or images, and parishioners were examined to determine whether they kept in their houses any object that could be connected with saint devotion. Such objects, reminders of the old, wrong teaching, had to be destroyed—they were not even allowed to be retained as keepsakes. The Reformers recognized that to overcome centuries of belief required drastic action.

One of the strongest arguments against saint-worship was that it was idolatry. Images were compared with the pagan idols mentioned and condemned in the Old Testament. Neither did it help when stubborn clergy, in defence of their tradition, used words such as "veneration", "service" or "honour" instead of "worship": the practice still amounted to idolatry. Reformers would quote the second commandment as their authority for destroying the statues and images.

As well as the serious charge of idolatry, much of the criticism of images came from the fact that it was sheer foolishness. Not only were there enough examples of fraudulent relics to give this kind of argument a solid basis, but even the genuine relics were dismissed as having no value. Saints could not answer prayers. God is the one who looks down from heaven and answers prayers—why not pray to him? It makes much more sense to make requests of the one who hears and acts. "Regarding the saints", Calvin wrote, "… if we attribute any prayer to them, let us not even dream that they have any other way to petition God than through Christ, who alone is the way". This view relies on the Reformers' doctrine of access to God in and through Jesus Christ, in the Spirit. This brought a much more close and direct relationship to God than the medieval church allowed. In Reformation doctrine, a Christian was as close to God as Christ himself, and so had no need of a saint as a mediator: what is more, the saint, being only another Christian, had no special privilege with God above any other Christian. Pilgrimages, then, were simple foolishness: what benefit was there in them?

In the Reformers' view, saints were not to be worshipped because they were not divine, nor did they have a privileged contact with the divine. They were not mediators, for the Reformers allowed only one mediator, Christ. The Reformers' doctrine, then, removed the distinction between saints and other Christians. The saints did not have the power to heal their fellow-Christians in a supernatural way, for the saints were no closer to the divine than any other Christian. The strong claim of 'faith alone' left no room for gradations of holiness, and particularly no room for some Christians to be so holy that they could bring God's power to bear in the natural world in such spectacular ways. There was therefore no such thing as a 'saint', in any sense that distinguished one Christian from another; all Christians were saints, and the Reformers vehemently upheld this spiritual equality.

3 A changing world

The Reformers simplified liturgy; they destroyed the shrines of saints; they cut down the elaborate ceremonies of traditional devotion, creating a more basic order of church service. They criticized superstition, as they judged medieval ceremonialism to be, and they removed what they considered magical, an undue attention given to external forms and ritual. They stripped churches of their decorations, vestments and chalices; they removed images, devotional candles, screens and windows; they banned ceremonies and rigorously dragged their various churches into uniform devotional practices.

These things are all true, and you will find them described in any number of secular histories of the Reformation. However, on its own this description is incomplete. The Reformation was not solely, or even primarily, a negative movement. The Reformers only desired to destroy existing structures insofar as they interfered with the establishment of the new structures, new worship, new liturgy—indeed, a new religion, which was a return to the religion of the Bible.

We could even think of the Reformers as missionaries rather than reformers; they had a message that was radically different in content and practical implications from the religion of late medieval Europe.

They had a different view of humanity. They preached that every man was born into a state of complete sin, and had no recourse by his own power to escape this sin. Good deeds done in this state did not count for any favour with God. Humans could, however, be rescued by God from this state. This rescue was achieved entirely by God's power and depended not at all on the effort of the human. The human side was experienced as depending on God's mercy, when the message of the gospel was heard. In Tyndale's language, God had promised to rescue his people from sin, and he kept his promise: the human part was merely believing the promise, and acknowledging that God had both the power and the faithfulness to keep it. Humans could not change their own spiritual state, regardless of any moral or religious activities they may undertake. Even the act of believing the promise was regarded as a gift from God, an unmerited act of his grace through the work of the Holy Spirit.

Once regenerated by this work of the Spirit, and with their faith only in God, all Christians were expected to work at obedience to God in their own lives, but not to pride themselves on holiness. All Christians, in the Reformers' view, were equally close to God, which was as close to God as it was possible to be. All had become children of God, members of his very family, as well as citizens of the kingdom of heaven. There were no gradations of holiness—all were saints, all were priests. The state of holiness had been imparted freely and completely by God, and no human gained more of it than another. Obedience was very important as a true acceptance of God's grace, and so the Reformers constantly encouraged their people to godly behaviour, honesty, charity and so on. However, one's level of obedience made no essential difference to where one stood with God. Since all Christians are freely forgiven by God's grace in Christ, which they receive by simple trust alone, one did not progress up some spiritual pecking order to 'sainthood' by virtue of one's good works. Human beings in the Reformers' world were plain folk, and had to be content with a spiritual equality—which meant they could be confident that there were no hidden mysteries obtainable only by the few.

Consequently, the medieval (and neoplatonic) idea of a hierarchy of beings, stretching from the physical through the supernatural realms to God, was replaced by a far less complicated picture. God reigned supreme, and his primary activity in the world was to speak his Word and to bring people to an understanding of and obedience to it. The devil tried to undermine this activity, by interfering in human affairs and engaging in various deceptive activities.

But it was not a magical battle, to be waged by the incantation of formulae, or the protection of sacred charms. The spiritual battle was no longer a clash between evil forces and the powerful physical objects that could protect against them; spiritual warfare was a battle of education against ignorance. It was a shift in ideas in which humans became far less passive. They were able to bring to bear on the battle their own internal powers of understanding and rationality, rather than relying on external and inexplicable powers of bells or holy water. The universe came to be more intelligible, with a God who wished for understanding, not mysticism, and supernatural adversaries who could be dealt with through a simple trust in God's promises in Scripture.

The new view of God and his universe meant a radical change in perception of ritual objects. The holiness of holy water and holy oil, if they were 'holy', came from their use. Water and oil may well be used for religious purposes, but doing so did not indicate any essential change in what they *were*: it was merely a matter of use.

Fundamentally, the Reformation preached a view of God in which relationship with God was not achieved by ritual practices. The way of reaching God involved understanding a message, trusting it and thereby trusting the one who spoke it, and obeying the consequences of the message in real life. These were internal actions of mind and will. Holiness was worked out in attitude and obedience: it was not given or produced by ceremony. Some liturgies and rituals were retained but only for the sake of order in the church, not because they had any religious power in themselves.

Perhaps the most important part of the Reformers' theology, both for them and for our understanding of their world view, was their insistence on the absolute and complete love of God as Father. He did all that was necessary for salvation. There was no bargaining, for God was prepared to do it all. He did not merely make it possible to enter heaven, conditional upon certain holy activities during life: he brought people into heaven, so they could be confident they were there now, while still alive. This doctrine was the Reformers' most basic argument for trust in God. It was not just that he provided all that was necessary for life—food, shelter, the whole of creation; their argument was that he was wholly devoted to the interests of his people, as demonstrated by his willingness to provide free salvation, although it was so costly to himself. The power of this confidence bursts from the Reformers' writings. It is the positive thrust of their message that inspired and made sense of their negative condemnations of medieval religion. They condemned such things, not simply because they were wrong, but because there was no need for them in this new, confident world of biblical Christianity.

The Reformation was more than an alteration of liturgical and ceremonial practice; it was a new way of looking at the world, which invaded every parish church and the daily life of every parishioner. There was more than a change in 'religion'; it was a change in thought, in life, and in what it meant to be a human being in God's world. It was a world in which we can have confidence in God and hope for the future, based on his grace to us in the Christ of the Scriptures, which we receive through faith alone.

Too often since then, these certainties have been attacked and eroded, and continue to be attacked today. Indeed, many Christians are ignorant of the issues, and do not realize that the truths for which the Reformers fought and died are as much under threat now as they were then. Many errors of Roman Catholicism remain uncorrected. Mystical, magical and superstitious versions of Christianity keep re-emerging in different forms.

We do not need to copy the Reformers out of love for history or tradition; yet we need to learn the lessons of the Reformation, and be reminded that the truth that inspired that generation to protest, and to reform, is still true today.

Part IV

Classics
of the
Reformation

LUTHER ON FREEDOM

$\mathfrak{A}$re we saved by our good works? Martin Luther, the man credited with starting the Reformation, struggled as a young monk with the knowledge that he failed to be perfectly godly. Through reading Romans he came to the great realization that his failure did not keep him from salvation, because salvation had been achieved by Christ. In understanding this, Luther began the preaching and writing that snowballed into a major religious upheaval throughout Europe. Largely through Luther, people came to see that the medieval church was not teaching the truth of the Christian gospel. In a movement that gathered momentum in a remarkably short time, people from all classes heard that the ceremonies, penances and religious works prescribed by the church were not the way to salvation; rather, heaven comes through trusting in Christ's death which paid for sin in a way that penance never could.

Luther wrote the 'The freedom of a Christian' as one of his last attempts to reconcile Rome to his teaching. He circulated it in an effort to explain his teaching and demonstrate its essential soundness, as well as proving that it came from the Bible. This essay therefore contains in summary the message that Luther was trying to communicate to the church he loved. In it he demonstrates that we are completely saved by grace alone, removed from bondage and made totally free from any necessity of works of the law. As well as this, he answers the accusation that so often follows such a declaration: are Christians then free to sin and disobey God? Luther provides a beautifully clear and succinct demonstration of the place of godliness in the life of the free Christian.

The other essay in this section, 'Two kinds of righteousness', was originally published as a sermon, probably in 1519. The passionate common sense of this sermon is typical of Luther— as inspiring today as it was then.

A treatise on Christian liberty
(The freedom of a Christian)
by Martin Luther

Many people have considered Christian faith an easy thing, and not a few have given it a place among the virtues. They do this because they have not experienced it and have never tasted the great strength there is in faith. It is impossible to write well about it or to understand what has been written about it unless one has at one time or another experienced the courage which faith gives a man when trials oppress him. But he who has had even a faint taste of it can never write, speak, meditate, or hear enough concerning it. It is a living "spring of water welling up to eternal life", as Christ calls it in John 4 [:14].

As for me, although I have no wealth of faith to boast of and know how scant my supply is, I nevertheless hope that I have attained to a little faith, even though I have been assailed by great and various temptations; and I hope that I can discuss it, if not more elegantly, certainly more to the point, than those literalists and subtle disputants have previously done, who have not even understood what they have written.

To make the way smoother for the unlearned—for only them do I serve—I shall set down the following two propositions concerning the freedom and the bondage of the spirit:

A Christian is a perfectly free lord of all, subject to none.

A Christian is a perfectly dutiful servant of all, subject to all.

These two theses seem to contradict each other. If, however, they should be found to fit together they would serve our purpose beautifully. Both are Paul's own statements, who says in 1 Cor 9 [:19], "For though I am free from all men, I have made myself a slave to all", and in Rom 13 [:8], "Owe no-one anything, except to love one another". Love by its very nature is ready to serve and be subject to him who is loved. So Christ, although he was Lord of all, was "born of woman, born under the law" [Gal 4:4], and therefore was at the same time a free man and a servant, "in the form of God" and "of a servant" [Phil 2:6-7].

Let us start, however, with something more remote from our subject, but more obvious. Man has a twofold nature, a spiritual and a bodily one. According to the spiritual nature, which men refer to as the soul, he is called a spiritual, inner, or new man. According to the bodily nature, which men refer to as flesh, he is called a carnal, outward, or old man, of whom the Apostle writes in 2 Cor 4 [:16], "Though our outer nature is wasting away, our inner nature is being renewed every day". Because of this diversity of nature the Scriptures assert contradictory things concerning the same man, since these two men in the same man contradict each other, "for the desires of the flesh are against the Spirit, and the desires of the Spirit are against the flesh", according to Gal 5 [:17].

First, let us consider the inner man to see how a righteous, free, and pious Christian—that is, a spiritual, new, and inner man—becomes what he is. It is evident that no external thing has any influence in producing Christian righteousness or freedom, or in producing unrighteousness or servitude. A simple argument will furnish the proof of this statement.

What can it profit the soul if the body is well, free, and active, and eats, drinks, and does as it pleases? For in these respects even the most godless slaves of vice may prosper. On the other hand, how will poor health or imprisonment or hunger or thirst or any other external misfortune harm the soul? Even the most godly men, and those who are free because of clear consciences, are afflicted with these things. None of these things touch either the freedom or the servitude of the soul. It does not help the soul if the body is adorned with the sacred robes of priests or dwells in sacred places or is occupied with sacred duties or prays, fasts, abstains from certain kinds of food, or does any work that can be done by the body and in the body. The righteousness and the freedom of the soul require something far different since the things which have been mentioned could be done by any wicked person. Such works produce nothing but hypocrites. On the other hand, it will not harm the soul if the body is clothed in secular dress, dwells in unconsecrated places, eats and drinks as others do, does not pray aloud, and neglects to do all the abovementioned things which hypocrites can do.

Furthermore, to put aside all kinds of works, even contemplation, meditation, and all that the soul can do, does not help. One thing, and only one thing, is necessary for Christian life, righteousness, and freedom. That one thing is the most holy Word of God, the gospel of Christ, as Christ says, John 11 [:25], "I am the resurrection and the life; he who believes in me, though he die, yet shall he live"; and John 8 [:36], "So if the Son makes you free, you will be free indeed"; and Matt 4 [:4], "Man shall not live by bread alone, but by every word that proceeds from the mouth of God". Let us then consider it certain and firmly established that the soul can do without anything except the Word of God and that where the Word of God is missing there is no help at all for the soul. If it has the Word of God it is rich and lacks nothing since it is the Word of life, truth, light, peace, righteousness, salvation, joy, liberty, wisdom, power, grace, glory, and of every incalculable blessing. This is why the prophet in the entire Psalm [119] and in many other places yearns and sighs for the Word of God and uses so many names to describe it.

On the other hand, there is no more terrible disaster with which the wrath of God can afflict men than a famine of the hearing of his Word, as he says in Amos [8:11]. Likewise there is no greater mercy than when he sends forth his Word, as we read in Psalm 107 [:20] : "He sent forth his word, and healed them, and delivered them from destruction". Nor was Christ sent into the world for any other ministry except that of the Word. Moreover, the entire spiritual estate—all the apostles, bishops, and priests—has been called and instituted only for the ministry of the Word.

You may ask, "What then is the Word of God, and how shall it be used, since there are so many words of God?" I answer: The Apostle explains this in Romans 1. The Word is the gospel of God concerning his Son, who was made flesh, suffered, rose from the dead, and was glorified through the Spirit who sanctifies. To preach Christ means to feed the soul, make it righteous, set it free, and save it, provided it believes the preaching. Faith alone is the saving and efficacious use of the Word of God, according to Rom 10 [:9]: "If you confess with your lips that Jesus is Lord and believe in your heart that God raised him from the dead, you will be saved". Furthermore, "Christ is the end of the law, that every one who has faith may be justified" [Rom 10:4]. Again, in Rom 1 [:17], "He who through faith is righteous shall live". The Word of God cannot be received and cherished by any works whatever but only by faith. Therefore it is clear that, as the soul needs only the Word of God for its life and righteousness, so it is justified by faith alone and not any works; for if it could be justified by anything else, it would not need the Word, and consequently it would not need faith.

This faith cannot exist in connection with works—that is to say, if you at the same time claim to be justified by works, whatever their character—for that would be the same as "limping with two different opinions" [1 Kgs 18:21], as worshipping Baal and kissing one's own hand [Job 31:27-28], which, as Job says, is a very great iniquity. Therefore the moment you begin to have faith you learn that all things in you are altogether blameworthy, sinful, and damnable, as the Apostle says in Rom 3 [:23], "Since all have sinned and fall short of the glory of God", and, "None is righteous, no, not one; ... all have turned aside, together they have gone wrong", Rom 3 [:10-12]. When you have learned this you will know that you need Christ, who suffered and rose again for you so that, if you believe in him, you may through this faith become a new man in so far as your sins are forgiven and you are justified by the merits of another, namely, of Christ alone.

Since, therefore, this faith can rule only in the inner man, as Rom 10 [:10] says, "For man believes with his heart and so is justified", and since faith alone justifies, it is clear that the inner man cannot be justified, freed, or saved by any outer work or action at all, and that these works, whatever their character, have nothing to do with this inner man. On the other hand, only ungodliness and unbelief of heart, and no outer work, make him guilty and a damnable servant of sin. Wherefore it ought to be the first concern of every Christian to lay aside all confidence in works and increasingly to strengthen faith alone and through faith to grow in the knowledge, not of works, but of Christ Jesus, who suffered and rose for him, as Peter teaches in the last chapter of his first Epistle, 1 Pet [5:10]. No other work makes a Christian. Thus when the Jews asked Christ, as related in John 6 [:28], what they must do "to be doing the work of God", he brushed aside the multitude of works which he saw they did in great profusion and suggested one work, saying, "This is the work of God, that you believe in him whom he has sent" [John 6:29]; "for on him has God the Father set his seal" [John 6:27].

Therefore true faith in Christ is a treasure beyond comparison which brings with it complete salvation and saves man from every evil, as Christ says in the last chapter of Mark [16:16]: "He who believes and is baptized will be saved; but he who does not believe will be condemned". Isaiah contemplated this treasure and foretold it in chapter 10: "The Lord will make a small and consuming word upon the land, and it will overflow with righteousness" [cf. Isa 10:22]. This is as though he said, "Faith, which is a small and perfect fulfilment of the law, will fill believers with so great a righteousness that they will need nothing more to become righteous". So Paul says, Rom 10 [:10], "For man believes with his heart and so is justified".

Should you ask how it happens that faith alone justifies and offers us such a treasure of great benefits without works in view of the fact that so many works, ceremonies, and laws are prescribed in the Scriptures, I answer: First of all, remember what has been said, namely, that faith alone, without works, justifies, frees, and saves; we shall make this clearer later on. Here we must point out that the entire Scripture of God is divided into two parts: commandments and promises.

Although the commandments teach things that are good, the things taught are not done as soon as they are taught, for the commandments show us what we ought to do but do not give us the power to do it. They are intended to teach man to know himself, that through them he may recognize his inability to do good and may despair of his own ability. That is why they are called the Old Testament and constitute the Old Testament. For example, the commandment, "You shall not covet" [Exod 20:17], is a command which proves us all to be sinners, for no-one can avoid coveting no matter how much he may struggle against it. Therefore, in order not to covet and to fulfil the commandment, a man is compelled to despair of himself, to seek the help which he does not find in himself elsewhere and from someone else, as stated in Hos [13:9]: "Destruction is your own, O Israel: your help is only in me". As we fare with respect to one commandment, so we fare with all, for it is equally impossible for us to keep any one of them.

Now when a man has learned through the commandments to recognize his helplessness and is distressed about how he might satisfy the law—since the law must be fulfilled so that not a jot or tittle shall be lost, otherwise man will be condemned without hope—then, being truly humbled and reduced to nothing in his own eyes, he finds in himself nothing whereby he may be justified and saved. Here the second part of Scripture comes to our aid, namely, the promises of God which declare the glory of God, saying, "If you wish to fulfil the law and not covet, as the law demands, come, believe in Christ in whom grace, righteousness, peace, liberty, and all things are promised you. If you believe, you shall have all things; if you do not believe, you shall lack all things". That which is impossible for you to accomplish by trying to fulfil all the works of the law—many and useless as they all are—you will accomplish quickly and easily through faith. God our Father has made all things depend on faith so that whoever has faith will have everything, and whoever does not have faith will have nothing. "For God has consigned all men to disobedience, that he may have mercy upon all", as it is stated in Rom 11 [:32]. Thus the promises of God give what the commandments of God demand and fulfil what the law prescribes so that all things may be God's alone, both the commandments and the fulfilling of the commandments. He alone commands, he alone fulfils. Therefore the promises of God belong to the New Testament. Indeed, they are the New Testament.

Since these promises of God are holy, true, righteous, free, and peaceful words, full of goodness, the soul which clings to them with a firm faith will be so closely united with them and altogether absorbed by them that it not only will share in all their power but will be saturated and intoxicated by them. If a touch of Christ healed, how much more will this most tender spiritual touch, this absorbing of the Word, communicate to the soul all things that belong to the Word. This, then, is how through faith alone without works the soul is justified by the Word of God, sanctified, made true, peaceful, and free, filled with every blessing and truly made a child of God, as John 1 [:12] says: "But to all who ... believed in his name, he gave power to become children of God".

From what has been said it is easy to see from what source faith derives such great power and why a good work or all good works together cannot equal it. No good work can rely upon the Word of God or live in the soul, for faith alone and the Word of God rule in the soul. Just as the heated iron glows like fire because of the union of fire with it, so the Word imparts its qualities to the soul. It is clear, then, that a Christian has all that he needs in faith and needs no works to justify him; and if he has no need of works, he has no need of the law; and if he has no need of the law, surely he is free from the law. It is true that "the law is not laid down for the just" [1 Tim 1:9]. This is that Christian liberty, our faith, which does not induce us to live in idleness or wickedness but makes the law and works unnecessary for any man's righteousness and salvation.

This is the first power of faith. Let us now examine also the second. It is a further function of faith that it honours him whom it trusts with the most reverent and highest regard since it considers him truthful and trustworthy. There is no other honour equal to the estimate of truthfulness and righteousness with which we honour him whom we trust. Could we ascribe to a man anything greater than truthfulness and righteousness and perfect goodness? On the other hand, there is no way in which we can show greater contempt for a man than to regard him as false and wicked and to be suspicious of him, as we do when we do not trust him. So when the soul firmly trusts God's promises, it regards him as truthful and righteous. Nothing more excellent than this can be ascribed to God. The very highest worship of God is this: that we ascribe to him truthfulness, righteousness, and whatever else should be ascribed to one who is trusted. When this is done, the soul consents to his will. Then it hallows his name and allows itself to be treated according to God's good pleasure for, clinging to God's promises, it does not doubt that he who is true, just, and wise will do, dispose, and provide all things well.

Is not such a soul most obedient to God in all things by this faith? What commandment is there that such obedience has not completely fulfilled? What more complete fulfilment is there than obedience in all things? This obedience, however, is not rendered by works, but by faith alone. On the other hand, what greater rebellion against God, what greater wickedness, what greater contempt of God is there than not believing his promise? For what is this but to make God a liar or to doubt that he is truthful?—that is, to ascribe truthfulness to one's self but lying and vanity to God? Does not a man who does this deny God and set himself up as an idol in his heart? Then of what good are works done in such wickedness, even if they were the works of angels and apostles? Therefore God has rightly included all things, not under anger or lust, but under unbelief, so that they who imagine that they are fulfilling the law by doing the works of chastity and mercy required by the law (the civil and human virtues) might not be saved. They are included under the sin of unbelief and must either seek mercy or be justly condemned.

When, however, God sees that we consider him truthful and by the faith of our heart pay him the great honour which is due him, he does us that great honour of considering us truthful and righteous for the sake of our faith. Faith works truth and righteousness by giving God what belongs to him. Therefore God in turn glorifies our righteousness. It is true and just that God is truthful and just, and to consider and confess him to be so is the same as being truthful and just. Accordingly he says in 1 Sam 2 [:30], "Those who honour me I will honour, and those who despise me shall be lightly esteemed". So Paul says in Rom 4 [:3] that Abraham's faith "was reckoned to him as righteousness" because by it he gave glory most perfectly to God, and that for the same reason our faith shall be reckoned to us as righteousness if we believe.

The third incomparable benefit of faith is that it unites

the soul with Christ as a bride is united with her bridegroom. By this mystery, as the Apostle teaches, Christ and the soul become one flesh [Eph 5:31-32]. And if they are one flesh and there is between them a true marriage—indeed the most perfect of all marriages, since human marriages are but poor examples of this one true marriage—it follows that everything they have they hold in common, the good as well as the evil. Accordingly the believing soul can boast of and glory in whatever Christ has as though it were its own, and whatever the soul has Christ claims as his own. Let us compare these and we shall see inestimable benefits. Christ is full of grace, life, and salvation. The soul is full of sins, death, and damnation. Now let faith come between them and sins, death, and damnation will be Christ's, while grace, life, and salvation will be the soul's; for if Christ is a bridegroom, he must take upon himself the things which are his bride's and bestow upon her the things that are his. If he gives her his body and very self, how shall he not give her all that is his? And if he takes the body of the bride, how shall he not take all that is hers?

Here we have a most pleasing vision not only of communion but of a blessed struggle and victory and salvation and redemption. Christ is God and man in one person. He has neither sinned nor died, and is not condemned, and he cannot sin, die, or be condemned; his righteousness, life, and salvation are unconquerable, eternal, omnipotent. By the wedding ring of faith he shares in the sins, death, and pains of hell which are his bride's. As a matter of fact, he makes them his own and acts as if they were his own and as if he himself had sinned; he suffered, died, and descended into hell that he might overcome them all. Now since it was such a one who did all this, and death and hell could not swallow him up, these were necessarily swallowed up by him in a mighty duel; for his righteousness is greater than the sins of all men, his life stronger than death, his salvation more invincible than hell. Thus the believing soul by means of the pledge of its faith is free in Christ, its bridegroom, free from all sins, secure against death and hell, and is endowed with the eternal righteousness, life, and salvation of Christ its bridegroom. So he takes to himself a glorious bride, "without spot or wrinkle, cleansing her by the washing of water with the word" [cf. Eph 5:26-27] of life, that is, by faith in the Word of life, righteousness, and salvation. In this way he marries her in faith, steadfast love, and in mercies, righteousness, and justice, as Hos 2 [:19-20] says.

Who then can fully appreciate what this royal marriage means? Who can understand the riches of the glory of this grace? Here this rich and divine bridegroom Christ marries this poor, wicked harlot, redeems her from all her evil, and adorns her with all his goodness. Her sins cannot now destroy her, since they are laid upon Christ and swallowed up by him. And she has that righteousness in Christ, her husband, of which she may boast as of her own and which she can confidently display alongside her sins in the face of death and hell and say, "If I have sinned, yet my Christ, in whom I believe, has not sinned, and all his is mine and all mine is his", as the bride in the Song of Solomon [2:16] says, "My beloved is mine and I am his". This is what Paul means when he says in 1 Cor 15 [:57], "Thanks be to God, who gives us the victory through our Lord Jesus Christ," that is, the victory over sin and death, as he also says there, "The sting of death is sin, and the power of sin is the law" [1 Cor 15:56].

From this you once more see that much is ascribed to faith, namely, that it alone can fulfil the law and justify without works. You see that the First Commandment, which says, "You shall worship one God" is fulfilled by faith alone. Though you were nothing but good works from the soles of your feet to the crown of your head, you would still not be righteous or worship God or fulfil the First Commandment, since God cannot be worshipped unless you ascribe to him the glory of truthfulness and all goodness which is due him. This cannot be done by works but only by the faith of the heart. Not by the doing of works but by believing do we glorify God and acknowledge that he is truthful. Therefore faith alone is the righteousness of a Christian and the fulfilling of all the commandments, for he who fulfils the First Commandment has no difficulty in fulfilling all the rest.

But works, being inanimate things, cannot glorify God, although they can, if faith is present, be done to the glory of God. Here, however, we are not inquiring what works and what kind of works are done, but who it is that does them, who glorifies God and brings forth the works. This is done by faith which dwells in the heart and is the source and substance of all our righteousness. Therefore it is a blind and dangerous doctrine which teaches that the commandments must be fulfilled by works. The commandments must be fulfilled before any works can be done, and the works proceed from the fulfilment of the commandments [Rom 13:10], as we shall hear.

That we may examine more profoundly that grace which our inner man has in Christ, we must realize that in the Old Testament God consecrated to himself all the first-born males. The birthright was highly prized for it involved a twofold honour, that of priesthood and that of kingship. The firstborn brother was priest and lord over all the others and a type of Christ, the true and only firstborn of God the

Father and the Virgin Mary and true king and priest, but not after the fashion of the flesh and the world, for his kingdom is not of this world [John 18:36]. He reigns in heavenly and spiritual things and consecrates them—things such as righteousness, truth, wisdom, peace, salvation, etc. This does not mean that all things on earth and in hell are not also subject to him—otherwise how could he protect and save us from them?—but that his kingdom consists neither in them nor of them. Nor does his priesthood consist in the outer splendour of robes and postures like those of the human priesthood of Aaron and our present-day church; but it consists of spiritual things through which he by an invisible service intercedes for us in heaven before God, there offers himself as a sacrifice, and does all things a priest should do, as Paul describes him under the type of Melchizedek in the Epistle to the Hebrews [Heb 6-7]. Nor does he only pray and intercede for us but he teaches us inwardly through the living instruction of his Spirit, thus performing the two real functions of a priest, of which the prayers and the preaching of human priests are visible types.

Now just as Christ by his birthright obtained these two prerogatives, so he imparts them to and shares them with everyone who believes in him according to the law of the abovementioned marriage, according to which the wife owns whatever belongs to the husband. Hence all of us who believe in Christ are priests and kings in Christ, as 1 Pet 2 [:9] says: "You are a chosen race, God's own people, a royal priesthood, a priestly kingdom, that you may declare the wonderful deeds of him who called you out of darkness into his marvellous light".

The nature of this priesthood and kingship is something like this: First, with respect to the kingship, every Christian is by faith so exalted above all things that, by virtue of a spiritual power, he is lord of all things without exception, so that nothing can do him any harm. As a matter of fact, all things are made subject to him and are compelled to serve him in obtaining salvation. Accordingly Paul says in Rom 8 [:28], "All things work together for good for the elect", and in 1 Cor 3 [:21-23] "All things are yours whether … life or death or the present or the future, all are yours; and you are Christ's". This is not to say that every Christian is placed over all things to have and control them by physical power—a madness with which some churchmen are afflicted—for such power belongs to kings, princes, and other men on earth. Our ordinary experience in life shows us that we are subjected to all, suffer many things, and even die. As a matter of fact, the more Christian a man is, the more evils, sufferings, and deaths he must endure, as we see in Christ the firstborn prince himself, and in all his brethren, the saints. The power of which we speak is spiritual. It rules in the midst of enemies and is powerful in the midst of oppression. This means nothing else than that "power is made perfect in weakness" [2 Cor 12:9] and that in all things I can find profit toward salvation [Rom 8:28], so that the cross and death itself are compelled to serve me and to work together with me for my salvation. This is a splendid privilege and hard to attain, a truly omnipotent power, a spiritual dominion in which there is nothing so good and nothing so evil but that it shall work together for good to me, if only I believe. Yes, since faith alone suffices for salvation, I need nothing except faith exercising the power and dominion of its own liberty. Lo, this is the inestimable power and liberty of Christians.

Not only are we the freest of kings, we are also priests forever, which is far more excellent than being kings, for as priests we are worthy to appear before God to pray for others and to teach one another divine things. These are the functions of priests, and they cannot be granted to any unbeliever. Thus Christ has made it possible for us, provided we believe in him, to be not only his brethren, co-heirs, and fellow-kings, but also his fellow-priests. Therefore we may boldly come into the presence of God in the spirit of faith [Heb 10:19, 22] and cry "Abba, Father!", pray for one another, and do all things which we see done and foreshadowed in the outer and visible works of priests.

He, however, who does not believe is not served by anything. On the contrary, nothing works for his good, but he himself is a servant of all, and all things turn out badly for him because he wickedly uses them to his own advantage and not to the glory of God. So he is no priest but a wicked man whose prayer becomes sin and who never comes into the presence of God because God does not hear sinners [John 9:31]. Who then can comprehend the lofty dignity of the Christian? By virtue of his royal power he rules over all things, death, life, and sin, and through his priestly glory is omnipotent with God because he does the things which God asks and desires, as it is written, "He will fulfil the desire of those who fear him; he also will hear their cry and save them" [cf. Phil 4:13]. To this glory a man attains, certainly not by any works of his, but by faith alone.

From this anyone can clearly see how a Christian is free from all things and over all things so that he needs no works to make him righteous and save him, since faith alone abundantly confers all these things. Should he grow so foolish, however, as to presume to become righteous, free, saved, and a Christian by means of some good work, he would instantly lose faith and all its benefits, a foolishness aptly illustrated in the fable of the dog who runs along a stream with a piece of meat in his mouth and, deceived by the reflection of the meat in the water, opens his mouth to snap at it and so loses both the meat and the reflection.

You will ask, "If all who are in the church are priests, how do these whom we now call priests differ from laymen?" I answer: Injustice is done to those words 'priest', 'cleric', 'spiritual', 'ecclesiastic', when they are transferred from all Christians to those few who are now by a mischievous usage called 'ecclesiastics'. Holy Scripture makes no distinction between them, although it gives the name 'ministers', 'servants', 'stewards' to those who are now proudly called popes, bishops, and lords and who should according to the ministry of the Word serve others and teach them the faith of Christ and the freedom of believers. Although we are all equally priests, we cannot all publicly minister and teach. We ought not do so even if we could. Paul writes accordingly in 1 Cor 4 [:1], "This is how one should regard us, as servants of Christ and stewards of the mysteries of God". That stewardship, however, has now been developed into so great a display of power and so terrible a tyranny that no heathen empire or other earthly power can be compared with it, just as if laymen were not also Christians. Through this perversion the knowledge of Christian grace, faith, liberty, and of Christ himself has altogether perished, and its place has been taken by an unbearable bondage of human works and laws until we have become, as the Lamentations of Jeremiah [1] say, servants of the vilest men on earth who abuse our misfortune to serve only their base and shameless will.

To return to our purpose, I believe that it has now become clear that it is not enough or in any sense Christian to preach the works, life, and words of Christ as historical facts, as if the knowledge of these would suffice for the conduct of life; yet this is the fashion among those who must today be regarded as our best preachers. Far less is it sufficient or Christian to say nothing at all about Christ and to teach instead the laws of men and the decrees of the fathers. Now there are not a few who preach Christ and read about him that they may move men's affections to sympathy with Christ, to anger against the Jews, and such childish and effeminate nonsense. Rather ought Christ to be preached to the end that faith in him may be established that he may not only be Christ, but be Christ for you and me, and that what is said of him and is denoted in his name may be effectual in us. Such faith is produced and preserved in us by preaching why Christ came, what he brought and bestowed, what benefit it is to us to accept him. This is done when that Christian liberty which he bestows is rightly taught and we are told in what way we Christians are all kings and priests and therefore lords of all, and may firmly believe that whatever we have done is pleasing and acceptable in the sight of God, as I have already said.

What man is there whose heart, upon hearing these things, will not rejoice to its depth, and when receiving such comfort will not grow tender so that he will love Christ as he never could by means of any laws or works? Who would have the power to harm or frighten such a heart? If the knowledge of sin or the fear of death should break in upon it, it is ready to hope in the Lord. It does not grow afraid when it hears tidings of evil. It is not disturbed when it sees its enemies. This is so because it believes that the righteousness of Christ is its own and that its sin is not its own, but Christ's, and that all sin is swallowed up by the righteousness of Christ. This, as has been said above, is a necessary consequence on account of faith in Christ. So the heart learns to scoff at death and sin and to say with the Apostle; "O death, where is thy victory? O death, where is thy sting? The sting of death is sin, and the power of sin is the law. But thanks be to God, who gives us the victory through our Lord Jesus Christ" [1 Cor 15:55-57]. Death is swallowed up not only in the victory of Christ but also by our victory, because through faith his victory has become ours and in that faith we also are conquerors.

Let this suffice concerning the inner man, his liberty, and the source of his liberty, the righteousness of faith. He needs neither laws nor good works but, on the contrary, is injured by them if he believes that he is justified by them.

Now let us turn to the second part, the outer man. Here we shall answer all those who, offended by the word 'faith' and by all that has been said, now ask, "If faith does all things and is alone sufficient unto righteousness, why then are good works commanded? We will take our ease and do no works and be content with faith". I answer: not so, you wicked men, not so. That would indeed be proper if we were wholly inner and perfectly spiritual men. But such we shall be only at the last day, the day of the resurrection of the dead. As long as we live in the flesh we only begin to make some progress in that which shall be perfected in the future life. For this reason the Apostle in Rom 8 [:23] calls all that we attain in this life "the first fruits of the Spirit" because we shall indeed receive the greater portion, even the fullness of the Spirit, in the future. This is the place to assert that which was said above, namely, that a Christian is the servant of all and made subject to all. Insofar as he is free he does no works, but insofar as he is a servant he does all kinds of works. How this is possible we shall see.

Although, as I have said, a man is abundantly and sufficiently justified by faith inwardly, in his spirit, and so has all that he needs, except insofar as this faith and these riches must grow from day to day even to the future life; yet he remains in this mortal life on earth. In this life he must control his own body and have dealings with men. Here the works begin; here a man cannot enjoy leisure; here he must indeed take care to discipline his body by fastings, watchings, labours, and other reasonable discipline and to subject it to the Spirit so that it will obey and conform to the inner man and faith and not revolt against faith and hinder the inner man, as it is the nature of the body to do if it is not held in check. The inner man, who by faith is created in the image of God, is both joyful and happy because of Christ in whom so many benefits are conferred upon him; and therefore it is his one occupation to serve God joyfully and without thought of gain, in love that is not constrained.

While he is doing this, behold, he meets a contrary will in his own flesh which strives to serve the world and seeks its own advantage. This the spirit of faith cannot tolerate, but with joyful zeal it attempts to put the body under control and hold it in check, as Paul says in Rom 7 [:22-23], "For I delight in the law of God, in my inmost self, but I see in my members another law at war with the law of my mind and making me captive to the law of sin", and in another place, "But I pommel my body and subdue it, lest after preaching to others I myself should be disqualified" [1 Cor 9:27], and in Gal [5:24], "And those who belong to Christ Jesus have crucified the flesh with its passions and desires".

In doing these works, however, we must not think that a man is justified before God by them, for faith, which alone is righteousness before God, cannot endure that erroneous opinion. We must, however, realize that these works reduce the body to subjection and purify it of its evil lusts, and our whole purpose is to be directed only toward the driving out of lusts. Since by faith the soul is cleansed and made to love God, it desires that all things, and especially its own body, shall be purified so that all things may join with it in loving and praising God. Hence a man cannot be idle, for the need of his body drives him and he is compelled to do many good works to reduce it to subjection. Nevertheless the works themselves do not justify him before God, but he does the works out of spontaneous love in obedience to God and considers nothing except the approval of God, whom he would most scrupulously obey in all things.

In this way everyone will easily be able to learn for himself the limit and discretion, as they say, of his bodily castigations, for he will fast, watch, and labour as much as he finds sufficient to repress the lasciviousness and lust of his body. But those who presume to be justified by works do not regard the mortifying of the lusts, but only the works themselves, and think that if only they have done as many and as great works as are possible, they have done well and have become righteous. At times they even addle their brains and destroy, or at least render useless, their natural strength with their works. This is the height of folly and utter ignorance of Christian life and faith, that a man should seek to be justified and saved by works and without faith.

In order to make that which we have said more easily understood, we shall explain by analogies. We should think of the works of a Christian who is justified and saved by faith because of the pure and free mercy of God, just as we would think of the works which Adam and Eve did in Paradise, and all their children would have done if they had not sinned. We read in Gen 2 [:15] that "The Lord God took the man and put him in the garden of Eden to till it and keep it". Now

Adam was created righteous and upright and without sin by God so that he had no need of being justified and made upright through his tilling and keeping the garden; but, that he might not be idle, the Lord gave him a task to do, to cultivate and protect the garden. This task would truly have been the freest of works, done only to please God and not to obtain righteousness, which Adam already had in full measure and which would have been the birthright of us all.

The works of a believer are like this. Through his faith he has been restored to Paradise and created anew, has no need of works that he may become or be righteous; but that he may not be idle and may provide for and keep his body, he must do such works freely only to please God. Since, however, we are not wholly recreated, and our faith and love are not yet perfect, these are to be increased, not by external works, however, but of themselves.

A second example: A bishop, when he consecrates a church, confirms children, or performs some other duty belonging to his office, is not made a bishop by these works. Indeed, if he had not first been made a bishop, none of these works would be valid. They would be foolish, childish, and farcical. So the Christian who is consecrated by his faith does good works, but the works do not make him holier or more Christian, for that is the work of faith alone. And if a man were not first a believer and a Christian, all his works would amount to nothing and would be truly wicked and damnable sins.

The following statements are therefore true: "Good works do not make a good man, but a good man does good works; evil works do not make a wicked man, but a wicked man does evil works". Consequently it is always necessary that the substance or person himself be good before there can be any good works, and that good works follow and proceed from the good person, as Christ also says, "A good tree cannot bear evil fruit, nor can a bad tree bear good fruit" [Matt 7:18]. It is clear that the fruits do not bear the tree and that the tree does not grow on the fruits; also that, on the contrary, the trees bear the fruits and the fruits grow on the trees. As it is necessary, therefore, that the trees exist before their fruits and the fruits do not make trees either good or bad, but rather as the trees are, so are the fruits they bear; so a man must first be good or wicked before he does a good or wicked work, and his works do not make him good or wicked, but he himself makes his works either good or wicked.

Illustrations of the same truth can be seen in all trades. A good or a bad house does not make a good or a bad builder; but a good or a bad builder makes a good or a bad house. And in general, the work never makes the workman like itself, but the workman makes the work like himself. So it is with the works of man. As the man is, whether believer or unbeliever, so also is his work—good if it was done in faith, wicked if it was done in unbelief. But the converse is not true, that the work makes the man either a believer or an unbeliever. As works do not make a man a believer, so also they do not make him righteous. But as faith makes a man a believer and righteous, so faith does good works. Since, then, works justify no-one, and a man must be righteous before he does a good work, it is very evident that it is faith alone which, because of the pure mercy of God through Christ and in his Word, worthily and sufficiently justifies and saves the person. A Christian has no need of any work or law in order to be saved since through faith he is free from every law and does everything out of pure liberty and freely. He seeks neither benefit nor salvation since he already abounds in all things and is saved through the grace of God because in his faith he now seeks only to please God.

Furthermore, no good work helps justify or save an unbeliever. On the other hand, no evil work makes him wicked or damns him; but the unbelief which makes the person and the tree evil does the evil and damnable works. Hence when a man is good or evil, this is effected not by the works, but by faith or unbelief, as the Wise Man says, "This is the beginning of sin, that a man falls away from God" [cf. Sirach 10:14-15],[1] which happens when he does not believe. And Paul says in Heb 11 [:6], "For whoever would draw near to God must believe ..." And Christ says the same: "Either make the tree good, and its fruit good; or make the tree bad, and its fruit bad" [Matt 12:33], as if he would say, "Let him who wishes to have good fruit begin by planting a good tree". So let him who wishes to do good works begin not with the doing of works, but with believing, which makes the person good, for nothing makes a man good except faith, or evil except unbelief.

It is indeed true that in the sight of men a man is made good or evil by his works; but this being made good or evil only means that the man who is good or evil is pointed out and known as such, as Christ says in Matt 7 [:20], "Thus you will know them by their fruits". All this remains on the surface, however, and very many have been deceived by this outward appearance and have presumed to write and teach concerning good works by which we may be justified without even mentioning faith. They go their way, always being

1.   The apocryphal 'Book of Sirach' is listed in Article VI of the *Thirty-Nine Articles* of the Church of England as a book to be read for the example of life and instructions of manners, but not to establish any doctrine.

deceived and deceiving [2 Tim 3:13], progressing, indeed, but into a worse state, blind leaders of the blind, wearying themselves with many works and still never attaining to true righteousness [Matt 15:14]. Of such people Paul says in 2 Tim 3 [:5, 7], "Holding the form of religion but denying the power of it … who will listen to anybody and can never arrive at a knowledge of the truth".

Whoever, therefore, does not wish to go astray with those blind men must look beyond works, and beyond laws and doctrines about works. Turning his eyes from works, he must look upon the person and ask how he is justified. For the person is justified and saved, not by works or laws, but by the Word of God, that is, by the promise of his grace, and by faith, that the glory may remain God's, who saved us not by works of righteousness which we have done [Titus 3:5], but by virtue of his mercy by the word of his grace when we believed [1 Cor 1:21].

From this it is easy to know how far good works are to be rejected or not, and by what standard all the teachings of men concerning works are to be interpreted. If works are sought after as a means to righteousness, are burdened with this perverse leviathan, and are done under the false impression that through them one is justified, they are made necessary and freedom and faith are destroyed; and this addition to them makes them no longer good but truly damnable works. They are not free, and they blaspheme the grace of God since to justify and to save by faith belongs to the grace of God alone. What the works have no power to do they nevertheless—by a godless presumption through this folly of ours—pretend to do and thus violently force themselves to the office and glory of grace. We do not, therefore, reject good works; on the contrary, we cherish and teach them as much as possible. We do not condemn them for their own sake but on account of this godless addition to them and the perverse idea that righteousness is to be sought through them; for that makes them appear good outwardly, when in truth they are not good. They deceive men and lead them to deceive one another like ravening wolves in sheep's clothing [Matt 7:15].

But this leviathan, or perverse notion concerning works, is unconquerable where sincere faith is wanting. Those work-saints cannot get rid of it unless faith, its destroyer, comes and rules in their hearts. Nature of itself cannot drive it out or even recognize it, but rather regards it as a mark of the most holy will. If the influence of custom is added and confirms this perverseness of nature, as wicked teachers have caused it to do, it becomes an incurable evil and leads astray and destroys countless men beyond all hope of restoration. Therefore, although it is good to preach and write about penitence, confession, and satisfaction, our teaching is unquestionably deceitful and diabolical if we stop with that and do not go on to teach about faith.

Christ, like his forerunner John, not only said, "Repent" [Matt 3:2, 4:17], but added the word of faith, saying, "The kingdom of heaven is at hand". We are not to preach only one of these words of God, but both; we are to bring forth out of our treasure things new and old, the voice of the law as well as the word of grace [Matt 13:52]. We must bring forth the voice of the law that men may be made to fear and come to a knowledge of their sins and so be converted to repentance and a better life. But we must not stop with that, for that would only amount to wounding and not binding up, smiting and not healing, killing and not making alive, leading down into hell and not bringing back again, humbling and not exalting. Therefore we must also preach the word of grace and the promise of forgiveness by which faith is taught and aroused. Without this word of grace the works of the law, contrition, penitence, and all the rest are done and taught in vain.

Preachers of repentance and grace remain even to our day, but they do not explain God's law and promise that a man might learn from them the source of repentance and grace. Repentance proceeds from the law of God, but faith or grace from the promise of God, as Rom 10 [:17] says: "So faith comes from what is heard, and what is heard comes by the preaching of Christ". Accordingly man is consoled and exalted by faith in the divine promise after he has been humbled and led to a knowledge of himself by the threats and the fear of the divine law. So we read in Psalm 30 [:5]: "Weeping may tarry for the night, but joy comes with the morning".

Let this suffice concerning works in general and at the same time concerning the works which a Christian does for himself. Lastly, we shall also speak of the things which he does toward his neighbour. A man does not live for himself alone in this mortal body to work for it alone, but he lives also for all men on earth; rather, he lives only for others and not for himself. To this end he brings his body into subjection that he may the more sincerely and freely serve others, as Paul says in Rom 14 [:7-8], "None of us lives to himself, and none of us dies to himself. If we live, we live to the Lord, and if we die, we die to the Lord". He cannot ever in this life be idle and without works toward his neighbours, for he will necessarily speak, deal with, and exchange views with men, as Christ also, being made in the likeness of men [Phil 2:7], was found in form as a man and conversed with men, as

Baruch 3 [:38][2] says.

Man, however, needs none of these things for his righteousness and salvation. Therefore he should be guided in all his works by this thought and contemplate this one thing alone, that he may serve and benefit others in all that he does, considering nothing except the need and the advantage of his neighbour. Accordingly the Apostle commands us to work with our hands so that we may give to the needy, although he might have said that we should work to support ourselves. He says, however, "that he may be able to give to those in need" [Eph 4:28]. This is what makes caring for the body a Christian work, that through its health and comfort we may be able to work, to acquire, and lay by funds with which to aid those who are in need, that in this way the strong member may serve the weaker, and we may be sons of God, each caring for and working for the other, bearing one another's burdens and so fulfilling the law of Christ [Gal 6:2]. This is a truly Christian life. Here faith is truly active through love [Gal 5:6], that is, it finds expression in works of the freest service, cheerfully and lovingly done, with which a man willingly serves another without hope of reward; and for himself he is satisfied with the fullness and wealth of his faith.

Accordingly Paul, after teaching the Philippians how rich they were made through faith in Christ, in which they obtained all things, thereafter teaches them, saying, "So if there is any encouragement in Christ, any incentive of love, any participation in the Spirit, any affection and sympathy, complete my joy by being of the same mind, having the same

2.   Baruch was Jeremiah's scribe (see Jer 36:4); the apocryphal 'Book of Baruch' is attributed to him.

love, being in full accord and of one mind. Do nothing from selfishness or conceit, but in humility count others better than yourselves. Let each of you look not only to his own interests, but also to the interests of others" [Phil 2:1-4]. Here we see clearly that the Apostle has prescribed this rule for the life of Christians, namely, that we should devote all our works to the welfare of others, since each has such abundant riches in his faith that all his other works and his whole life are a surplus with which he can by voluntary benevolence serve and do good to his neighbour.

As an example of such life the Apostle cites Christ, saying, "Have this mind among yourselves, which you have in Christ Jesus, who, though he was in the form of God, did not count equality with God a thing to be grasped, but emptied himself, taking the form of a servant, being born in the likeness of men. And being found in human form he humbled himself and became obedient unto death" [Phil 2:5-8]. This salutary word of the Apostle has been obscured for us by those who have not at all understood his words, "form of God", "form of a servant", "human form", "likeness of men", and have applied them to the divine and the human nature. Paul means this: Although Christ was filled with the form of God and rich in all good things, so that he needed no work and no suffering to make him righteous and saved (for he had all this eternally), yet he was not puffed up by them and did not exalt himself above us and assume power over us, although he could rightly have done so; but, on the contrary, he so lived, laboured, worked, suffered, and died that he might be like other men and in fashion and in actions be nothing else than a man, just as if he had need of all these things and had nothing of the form of God. But he did all this for our sake, that he might serve us and that all things which he accomplished in this form of a servant might become ours.

So a Christian, like Christ his head, is filled and made rich by faith and should be content with this form of God which he has obtained by faith; only, as I have said, he should increase this faith until it is made perfect. For this faith is his life, his righteousness, and his salvation: it saves him and makes him acceptable, and bestows upon him all things that are Christ's, as has been said above, and as Paul asserts in Gal 2 [:20] when he says, "And the life I now live in the flesh I live by faith in the Son of God". Although the Christian is thus free from all works, he ought in this liberty to empty himself, take upon himself the form of a servant, be made in the likeness of men, be found in human form, and to serve, help, and in every way deal with his neighbour as he sees that God through Christ has dealt and still deals with him. This he should do freely, having regard for nothing but divine approval.

He ought to think: "Although I am an unworthy and condemned man, my God has given me in Christ all the riches of righteousness and salvation without any merit on my part, out of pure, free mercy, so that from now on I need nothing except faith which believes that this is true. Why should I not therefore freely, joyfully, with all my heart, and with an eager will do all things which I know are pleasing and acceptable to such a Father who has overwhelmed me with his inestimable riches? I will therefore give myself as a Christ to my neighbour, just as Christ offered himself to me; I will do nothing in this life except what I see is necessary, profitable, and salutary to my neighbour, since through faith I have an abundance of all good things in Christ."

Behold, from faith thus flow forth love and joy in the Lord, and from love a joyful, willing, and free mind that serves one's neighbour willingly and takes no account of gratitude or ingratitude, of praise or blame, of gain or loss. For a man does not serve that he may put men under obligations. He does not distinguish between friends and enemies or anticipate their thankfulness or unthankfulness, but he most freely and most willingly spends himself and all that he has, whether he wastes all on the thankless or whether he gains a reward. As his Father does, distributing all things to all men richly and freely, making "his sun rise on the evil and on the good" [Matt 5:45], so also the son does all things and suffers all things with that freely bestowing joy which is his delight when through Christ he sees it in God, the dispenser of such great benefits.

Therefore, if we recognize the great and precious things which are given us, as Paul says [Rom 5:5], our hearts will be filled by the Holy Spirit with the love which makes us free, joyful, almighty workers and conquerors over all tribulations, servants of our neighbours, and yet lords of all. For those who do not recognize the gifts bestowed upon them through Christ, however, Christ has been born in vain; they go their way with their works and shall never come to taste or feel those things. Just as our neighbour is in need and lacks that in which we abound, so we were in need before God and lacked his mercy. Hence, as our heavenly Father has in Christ freely come to our aid, we also ought freely to help our neighbour through our body and its works, and each one should become as it were a Christ to the other that we may be Christs to one another and Christ may be the same in all, that is, that we may be truly Christians.

Who then can comprehend the riches and the glory of the Christian life? It can do all things and has all things and lacks nothing. It is lord over sin, death, and hell, and yet at the same time it serves, ministers to, and benefits all men. But alas in our day this life is unknown throughout the world; it is neither preached about nor sought after; we are altogether ignorant of our own name and do not know why we are Christians or bear the name of Christians. Surely we are named after Christ, not because he is absent from us, but because he dwells in us, that is, because we believe in him and are Christs one to another and do to our neighbours as Christ does to us. But in our day we are taught by the doctrine of men to seek nothing but merits, rewards, and the things that are ours; of Christ we have made only a taskmaster far harsher than Moses.

We have a pre-eminent example of such a faith in the blessed Virgin. As is written in Luke 2 [:22], she was purified according to the law of Moses according to the custom of all women, although she was not bound by that law and did not need to be purified. Out of free and willing love, however, she submitted to the law like other women that she might not offend or despise them. She was not justified by this work, but being righteous she did it freely and willingly. So also our works should be done, not that we may be justified by them, since, being justified beforehand by faith, we ought to do all things freely and joyfully for the sake of others.

St Paul also circumcised his disciple Timothy, not because circumcision was necessary for his righteousness, but that he might not offend or despise the Jews who were weak in the faith and could not yet grasp the liberty of faith. But, on the other hand, when they despised the liberty of faith and insisted that circumcision was necessary for righteousness, he resisted them and did not allow Titus to be circumcised, Gal 2 [:3]. Just as he was unwilling to offend or despise any man's weak faith and yielded to their will for a time, so he was also unwilling that the liberty of faith should be offended against or despised by stubborn, work-righteous men. He chose a middle way, sparing the weak for a time, but always withstanding the stubborn, that he might convert all to the liberty of faith. What we do should be done with the same zeal to sustain the weak in faith, as in Rom 14 [:1]; but we should firmly resist the stubborn teachers of works. Of this we shall say more later.

Christ also, in Matt 17 [:24-27], when the tax money was demanded of his disciples, discussed with St Peter whether the sons of the king were not free from the payment of tribute, and Peter affirmed that they were. Nonetheless, Christ commanded Peter to go to the sea and said, "Not to give offence to them, go to the sea and cast a hook, and take the first fish that comes up, and when you open its mouth you will find a shekel; take that and give it to them for me and for yourself". This incident fits our subject beautifully for Christ here calls himself and those who are his children sons of the king, who need nothing; and yet he freely submits and pays the tribute. Just as necessary and helpful as this work was to Christ's righteousness or salvation, just so much do all other works of his or his followers avail for righteousness, since they all follow after righteousness and are free and are done only to serve others and to give them an example of good works.

Of the same nature are the precepts which Paul gives in Rom 13 [:1-7], namely, that Christians should be subject to the governing authorities and be ready to do every good work, not that they shall in this way be justified, since they already are righteous through faith, but that in the liberty of the Spirit they shall by so doing serve others and the authorities themselves and obey their will freely and out of love. The works of all colleges, monasteries, and priests should be of this nature. Each one should do the works of his profession and station, not that by them he may strive after righteousness, but that through them he may keep his body under control, be an example to others who also need to keep their bodies under control, and finally that by such works he may submit his will to that of others in the freedom of love. But very great care must always be exercised so that no man in a false confidence imagines that by such works he will be justified or acquire merit or be saved; for this is the work of faith alone, as I have repeatedly said.

Anyone knowing this could easily and without danger find his way through those numberless mandates and precepts of pope, bishops, monasteries, churches, princes, and magistrates upon which some ignorant pastors insist as if they were necessary to righteousness and salvation, calling them "precepts of the church", although they are nothing of the kind. For a Christian, as a free man, will say, "I will fast, pray, do this and that as men command, not because it is necessary to my righteousness or salvation; but that I may show due respect to the pope, the bishop, the community, a magistrate, or my neighbour, and give them an example. I will do and suffer all things, just as Christ did and suffered far more for me, although he needed nothing of it all for himself, and was made under the law for my sake, although he was not under the law". Although tyrants do violence or injustice in making their demands, yet it will do no harm as long as they demand nothing contrary to God.

From what has been said, everyone can pass a safe judgement on all works and laws and make a trustworthy distinction between them and know who are the blind and ignorant pastors and who are the good and true. Any work that is not done solely for the purpose of keeping the body under control or of serving one's neighbour, as long as he asks nothing contrary to God, is not good or Christian. For this reason I greatly fear that few or no colleges, monasteries, altars, and offices of the church are really Christian in our day—nor the special fasts and prayers on certain saints' days. I fear, I say, that in all these we seek only our profit, thinking that through them our sins are purged away and that we find salvation in them. In this way Christian liberty perishes altogether. This is a consequence of our ignorance of Christian faith and liberty.

This ignorance and suppression of liberty very many blind pastors take pains to encourage. They stir up and urge on their people in these practices by praising such works, puffing them up with their indulgences, and never teaching faith. If, however, you wish to pray, fast, or establish a foundation in the church, I advise you to be careful not to do it in order to obtain some benefit, whether temporal or eternal, for you would do injury to your faith which alone offers you all things. Your one care should be that faith may grow, whether it is trained by works or sufferings. Make your gifts freely and for no consideration, so that others may profit by them and fare well because of you and your goodness. In this way you shall be truly good and Christian. Of what benefit to you are the good works which you do not need for keeping your body under control? Your faith is sufficient for you, through which God has given you all things.

See, according to this rule the good things we have from God should flow from one to the other and be common to all, so that everyone should "put on" his neighbour and so conduct himself toward him as if he himself were in the other's place. From Christ the good things have flowed and are flowing into us. He has so "put on" us and acted for us as if he had been what we are. From us they flow on to those who have need of them so that I should lay before God my faith and my righteousness that they may cover and intercede for the sins of my neighbour which I take upon myself and so labour and serve in them as if they were my very own. That is what Christ did for us. This is true love and the genuine rule of a Christian life. Love is true and genuine where there is true and genuine faith. Hence the Apostle says of love in 1 Cor 13 [:5] that "it does not seek its own".

We conclude, therefore, that a Christian lives not in himself, but in Christ and in his neighbour. Otherwise he is not a Christian. He lives in Christ through faith, in his neighbour through love. By faith he is caught up beyond himself into God. By love he descends beneath himself into his neighbour. Yet he always remains in God and in his love, as Christ says in John 1 [:51], "Truly, truly, I say to you, you will see heaven opened, and the angels of God ascending and descending upon the Son of Man".

Enough now of freedom. As you see, it is a spiritual and true freedom and makes our hearts free from all sins, laws and commands, as Paul says, 1 Tim 1 [:9], "The law is not laid down for the just". It is more excellent than all other liberty, which is external, as heaven is more excellent than earth. May Christ give us this liberty both to understand and to preserve. Amen.

Finally, something must be added for the sake of those for whom nothing can be said so well that they will not spoil it by misunderstanding it. It is questionable whether they will understand even what will be said here. There are very many who, when they hear of this freedom of faith, immediately turn it into an occasion for the flesh and think that now all things are allowed them. They want to show that they are free men and Christians only by despising and finding fault with ceremonies, traditions, and human laws; as if they were Christians because on stated days they do not fast or eat meat when others fast, or because they do not use the accustomed prayers, and with upturned nose scoff at the precepts of men, although they utterly disregard all else that pertains to the Christian religion. The extreme opposite of these are those who rely for their salvation solely on their reverent observance of ceremonies, as if they would be saved because on certain days they fast or abstain from meats, or pray certain prayers; these make a boast of the precepts of the church and of the fathers, and do not care a fig for the things which are of the essence of our faith. Plainly, both are in error because they neglect the weightier things which are necessary to salvation, and quarrel so noisily about trifling and unnecessary matters.

How much better is the teaching of the Apostle Paul who bids us take a middle course and condemns both sides when he says, "Let not him who eats despise him who abstains, and let not him who abstains pass judgement on him who eats" [Rom 14:3]. Here you see that they who neglect and disparage ceremonies, not out of piety, but out of mere contempt, are reproved, since the Apostle teaches us not to despise them. Such men are puffed up by knowledge. On the other hand, he teaches those who insist on the ceremonies not to judge the others, for neither party acts toward the other according to the love that edifies. Wherefore we ought to listen to Scripture which teaches that we should not go aside to the right or to the left [Deut 28:14] but follow the statutes of the Lord which are right, "rejoicing the heart" [Ps 19:8]. As a man is not righteous because he keeps and clings to the works and forms of the ceremonies, so also will a man not be counted righteous merely because he neglects and despises them.

Our faith in Christ does not free us from works but from false opinions concerning works, that is, from the foolish presumption that justification is acquired by works. Faith redeems, corrects, and preserves our consciences so that we know that righteousness does not consist in works, although works neither can nor ought to be wanting; just as we cannot be without food and drink and all the works of this mortal body, yet our righteousness is not in them, but in faith; and yet those works of the body are not to be despised or neglected on that account. In this world we are bound by the needs of our bodily life, but we are not righteous because of them. "My kingship is not of this world" [John 18:36], says Christ. He does not, however, say, "My kingship is not here, that is, in this world". And Paul says, "Though we live in the world we are not carrying on a worldly war" [2 Cor 10:3], and in Gal 2 [:20], "The life I now live in the flesh I live by faith in the Son of God". Thus what we do, live, and are in works and ceremonies, we do because of the necessities of this life and of the effort to rule our body. Nevertheless we are righteous, not in these, but in the faith of the Son of God.

Hence the Christian must take a middle course and face those two classes of men. He will meet first the unyielding, stubborn ceremonialists who like deaf adders are not willing to hear the truth of liberty [Ps 58:4] but, having no faith, boast of, prescribe, and insist upon their ceremonies as means of justification. Such were the Jews of old, who were unwilling to learn how to do good. These he must resist, do the very opposite, and offend them boldly lest by their impious views they drag many with them into error. In the presence of such men it is good to eat meat, break the fasts, and for the sake of the liberty of faith do other things which they regard as the greatest of sins. Of them we must say, "Let them alone; they are blind guides". According to this principle Paul would not circumcise Titus when the Jews insisted that he should [Gal 2:3], and Christ excused the apostles when they plucked ears of grain on the Sabbath [Matt 12:1-8]. There are many similar instances. The other class of men whom a Christian will meet are the simple-minded, ignorant men, weak in the faith, as the Apostle calls them, who cannot yet grasp the liberty of faith, even if they were willing to do so [Rom 14:1]. These he must take care not to offend. He must yield to their weakness until they are more fully instructed. Since they do and think as they do, not because they are stubbornly wicked, but only because their faith is weak, the fasts and other things which they consider necessary must be observed to avoid giving them offence. This is the command of love which would harm no-one but would serve all men. It is not by their fault that they are weak, but by that of their pastors who have taken them captive with the snares of their traditions and have wickedly used these traditions as rods with which to beat them. They should have been delivered from these pastors by the teachings of faith and freedom. So the Apostle teaches us in Rom 14: "If food is a cause of my brother's falling, I will never eat meat" [cf. Rom 14:21 and 1 Cor 8:13]; and again, "I know and am persuaded in the Lord Jesus that nothing is unclean in itself; but it is unclean for any one who thinks it unclean" [Rom 14:14].

For this reason, although we should boldly resist those teachers of traditions and sharply censure the laws of the popes by means of which they plunder the people of God, yet we must spare the timid multitude whom those impious tyrants hold captive by means of these laws until they are set free. Therefore fight strenuously against the wolves, but for the sheep and not also against the sheep. This you will do if you inveigh against the laws and the lawgivers and at the same time observe the laws with the weak so that they will not be offended, until they also recognize tyranny and understand their freedom. If you wish to use your freedom, do so in secret, as Paul says, Rom 14 [:22], "The faith that you have, keep between yourself and God"; but take care not to use your freedom in the sight of the weak. On the other hand, use your freedom constantly and consistently in the sight of and despite the tyrants and the stubborn so that they also may learn that they are impious, that their laws are of no avail for righteousness, and that they had no right to set them up.

Since we cannot live our lives without ceremonies and works, and the perverse and untrained youth need to be restrained and saved from harm by such bonds; and since each one should keep his body under control by means of such works, there is need that the minister of Christ be far-seeing and faithful. He ought so to govern and teach Christians in all these matters that their conscience and faith will not be offended and that there will not spring up in them a suspicion and a root of bitterness and many will thereby be defiled, as Paul admonishes the Hebrews [Heb 12:15]; that is, that they may not lose faith and become defiled by the false estimate of the value of works and think that they must be justified by works. Unless faith is at the same time constantly taught, this happens easily and defiles a great many, as has been done until now through the pestilent, impious, soul-destroying traditions of our popes and the opinions of our theologians. By these snares numberless souls have been dragged down to hell, so that you might see in this the work of Antichrist.

In brief, as wealth is the test of poverty, business the test of faithfulness, honours the test of humility, feasts the test of temperance, pleasures the test of chastity, so ceremonies are the test of the righteousness of faith. "Can a man", asks Solomon, "carry fire in his bosom and his clothes and not be burned?" [Prov 6:27]. Yet as a man must live in the midst of wealth, business, honours, pleasures, and feasts, so also must he live in the midst of ceremonies, that is, in the midst of dangers. Indeed, as infant boys need beyond all else to be cherished in the bosoms and by the hands of maidens to keep them from perishing, yet when they are grown up their salvation is endangered if they associate with maidens, so the inexperienced and perverse youth need to be restrained and trained by the iron bars of ceremonies lest their unchecked ardour rush headlong into vice after vice. On the other hand, it would be death for them always to be held in bondage to ceremonies, thinking that these justify them. They are rather to be taught that they have been so imprisoned in ceremonies, not that they should be made righteous or gain great merit by them, but that they might thus be kept from doing evil and might more easily be instructed to the righteousness of faith. Such instruction they would not endure if the impulsiveness of their youth were not restrained.

Hence ceremonies are to be given the same place in the life of a Christian as models and plans have among builders and artisans. They are prepared, not as a permanent structure, but because without them nothing could be built or made. When the structure is complete the models and plans are laid aside. You see, they are not despised, rather they are greatly sought after; but what we despise is the false estimate of them since no-one holds them to be the real and permanent structure.

If any man were so flagrantly foolish as to care for nothing all his life long except the most costly, careful, and persistent preparation of plans and models and never to think of the structure itself, and were satisfied with his work in producing such plans and mere aids to work, and boasted of it, would not all men pity his insanity and think that something great might have been built with what he has wasted? Thus we do not despise ceremonies and works, but we set great store by them; but we despise the false estimate placed upon works in order that no-one may think that they are true righteousness, as those hypocrites believe who spend and lose their whole lives in zeal for works and never reach that goal for the sake of which the works are to be done, who, as the Apostle says, "will listen to anybody and can never arrive at a knowledge of the truth" [2 Tim 3:7]. They seem to wish to build, they make their preparations, and yet they never build. Thus they remain caught in the form of religion and do not attain unto its power [2 Tim 3:5]. Meanwhile they are pleased with their efforts and even dare to judge all others whom they do not see shining with a like show of works. Yet with the gifts of God which they have spent and abused in vain they might, if they had been filled with faith, have accomplished great things to their own salvation and that of others.

Since human nature and natural reason, as it is called, are by nature superstitious and ready to imagine, when laws and works are prescribed, that righteousness must be obtained through laws and works; and further, since they are trained and confirmed in this opinion by the practice of all earthly lawgivers, it is impossible that they should of themselves escape from the slavery of works and come to a knowledge of the freedom of faith. Therefore there is need of the prayer that the Lord may give us and make us theodidacti, that is, those taught by God [John 6:45], and himself, as he has promised, write his law in our hearts; otherwise there is no hope for us. If he himself does not teach our hearts this wisdom hidden in mystery [1 Cor 2:7], nature can only condemn it and judge it to be heretical because nature is offended by it and regards it as foolishness. So we see that it happened in the old days in the case of the apostles and prophets, and so godless and blind popes and their flatterers do to me and to those who are like me. May God at last be merciful to them and to us and cause his face to shine upon us that we may know his way upon earth [Ps 67:1-2], his salvation among all nations, God, who is blessed forever [2 Cor 11:31]. Amen.

Two kinds of righteousness

by Martin Luther

Brethren, "have this mind among yourselves, which you have in Christ Jesus, who, though he was in the form of God, did not count equality with God a thing to be grasped" [Phil 2:5-6].

There are two kinds of Christian righteousness, just as man's sin is of two kinds. The first is alien righteousness, that is the righteousness of another, instilled from without. This is the righteousness of Christ by which he justifies through faith, as it is written in 1 Cor 1 [:30]: "Whom God made our wisdom, our righteousness and sanctification and redemption". In John 11 [:25-26], Christ himself states: "I am the resurrection and the life; he who believes in me ... shall never die". Later he adds in John 14 [:6], "I am the way, and the truth, and the life". This righteousness, then, is given to men in baptism and whenever they are truly repentant. Therefore a man can with confidence boast in Christ and say: "Mine are Christ's living, doing, and speaking, his suffering and dying, mine as much as if I had lived, done, spoken, suffered, and died as he did". Just as a bridegroom possesses all that is his bride's and she all that is his—for the two have all things in common because they are one flesh [Gen 2:24]—so Christ and the church are one spirit [Eph 5:29-32]. Thus the blessed God and Father of mercies has, according to Peter, granted to us very great and precious gifts in Christ

[2 Pet 1:4]. Paul writes in 2 Cor 1 [:3]: "Blessed be the God and Father of our Lord Jesus Christ, the Father of mercies and God of all comfort, who has blessed us in Christ with every spiritual blessing in the heavenly places" [Eph 1:3].

This inexpressible grace and blessing was long ago promised to Abraham in Gen 12 [:3]: "And in thy seed (that is, in Christ) shall all the nations of the earth be blessed" [Gen 22:18]. Isaiah 9 [:6] says: "For to us a child is born, to us a son is given". "To us", it says, because he is entirely ours with all his benefits if we believe in him, as we read in Rom 8 [:32]: "He who did not spare his own Son but gave him up for us all, will he not also give us all things with him?" Therefore everything which Christ has is ours, graciously bestowed on us unworthy men out of God's sheer mercy, although we have rather deserved wrath and condemnation, and hell also. Even Christ himself, therefore, who says he came to do the most sacred will of his Father [John 6:38], became obedient to him; and whatever he did, he did it for us and desired it to be ours, saying, "I am among you as one who serves" [Luke 22:27]. He also states, "This is my body, which is given for you" [Luke 22:19]. Isaiah 43 [:24] says, "You have burdened me with your sins, you have wearied me with your iniquities".

Through faith in Christ, therefore, Christ's righteousness becomes our righteousness and all that he has becomes ours; rather, he himself becomes ours. Therefore the Apostle calls it "the righteousness of God" in Rom 1 [:17]: For in the gospel "the righteousness of God is revealed … ; as it is written, 'The righteous shall live by his faith'". Finally, in the same epistle, chapter 3 [:28], such a faith is called "the righteousness of God": "We hold that a man is justified by faith". This is an infinite righteousness, and one that swallows up all sins in a moment, for it is impossible that sin should exist in Christ. On the contrary, he who trusts in Christ exists in Christ; he is one with Christ, having the same righteousness as he. It is therefore impossible that sin should remain in him. This righteousness is primary; it is the basis, the cause, the source of all our own actual righteousness. For this is the righteousness given in place of the original righteousness lost in Adam. It accomplishes the same as that original righteousness would have accomplished; rather, it accomplishes more.

It is in this sense that we are to understand the prayer in Psalm 30 [Ps 31:1]: "In thee, O Lord, do I seek refuge; let me never be put to shame; in thy righteousness deliver me!" It does not say "in my" but "in thy righteousness", that is, in the righteousness of Christ my God which becomes ours through faith and by the grace and mercy of God. In many passages of the Psalter, faith is called "the work of the Lord", "confession", "power of God", "mercy", "truth", "righteousness". All these are names for faith in Christ, rather, for the righteousness which is in Christ. The Apostle therefore dares to say in Gal 2 [:20], "It is no longer I who live, but Christ who lives in me". He further states in Eph 3 [:14-17]: "I bow my knees before the Father ... that ... he may grant ... that Christ may dwell in your hearts through faith".

Therefore this alien righteousness, instilled in us without our works by grace alone—while the Father, to be sure, inwardly draws us to Christ—is set opposite original sin, likewise alien, which we acquire without our works by birth alone. Christ daily drives out the old Adam more and more in accordance with the extent to which faith and knowledge of Christ grow. For alien righteousness is not instilled all at once, but it begins, makes progress, and is finally perfected at the end through death.

The second kind of righteousness is our proper righteousness, not because we alone work it, but because we work with that first and alien righteousness. This is that manner of life spent profitably in good works, in the first place, in slaying the flesh and crucifying the desires with respect to the self, of which we read in Gal 5 [:24]: "And those who belong to Christ Jesus have crucified the flesh with its passions and desires". In the second place, this righteousness consists in love to one's neighbour, and in the third place, in meekness and fear toward God. The Apostle is full of references to these, as is all the rest of Scripture. He briefly summarizes everything, however, in Titus 2 [:12]: "In this world let us live soberly (pertaining to crucifying one's own flesh), justly (referring to one's neighbour), and devoutly (relating to God)".

This righteousness is the product of the righteousness of the first type, actually its fruit and consequence, for we read in Gal 5 [:22-23]: "But the fruit of the spirit [i.e. of a spiritual man, whose very existence depends on faith in Christ] is love, joy, peace, patience, kindness, goodness, faithfulness, gentleness, self-control". For because the works mentioned are works of men, it is obvious that in this passage a spiritual man is called "spirit". In John 3 [:6] we read: "That which is born of the flesh is flesh, and that which is born of the Spirit is spirit". This righteousness goes on to complete the first for it ever strives to do away with the old Adam and to destroy the body of sin. Therefore it hates itself and loves its neighbour; it does not seek its own good, but that of another, and in this its whole way of living consists. For in that it hates itself and does not seek its own, it crucifies the flesh. Because it seeks the good of another, it works love. Thus in each sphere it does God's will, living soberly with self, justly with neighbour, devoutly toward God.

This righteousness follows the example of Christ in this respect [1 Pet 2:21] and is transformed into his likeness [2 Cor 3:18]. It is precisely this that Christ requires. Just as he himself did all things for us, not seeking his own good but ours only—and in this he was most obedient to God the Father—so he desires that we also should set the same example for our neighbours.

We read in Rom 6 [:19] that this righteousness is set opposite our own actual sin: "For just as you once yielded your members to impurity and to greater and greater iniquity, so now yield your members to righteousness for sanctification". Therefore through the first righteousness arises the voice of the bridegroom who says to the soul, "I am yours", but through the second comes the voice of the bride who answers, "I am yours". Then the marriage is consummated; it becomes strong and complete in accordance with the Song of Solomon [2:16]: "My beloved is mine and I am his". Then the soul no longer seeks to be righteous in and for itself, but it has Christ as its righteousness and therefore seeks only the welfare of others. Therefore the Lord of the Synagogue threatens through the Prophet, "And I will make to cease from the cities of Judah and from the streets of Jerusalem the voice of mirth and the voice of gladness, the voice of the bridegroom and the voice of the bride" [Jer 7:34].

This is what the text we are now considering says: "Let this mind be in you, which was also in Christ Jesus" [Phil 2:5]. This means you should be as inclined and disposed toward one another as you see Christ was disposed toward you. How? Thus, surely, that "though he was in the form of God, [he] did not count equality with God a thing to be grasped, but emptied himself, taking the form of a servant" [Phil 2:6-7]. The term "form of God" here does not mean the "essence of God" because Christ never emptied himself of this. Neither can the phrase "form of a servant" be said to mean "human essence". But the "form of God" is wisdom, power, righteousness, goodness—and freedom too; for Christ was a free, powerful, wise man, subject to none of the vices or sins to which all other men are subject. He was pre-eminent in such attributes as are particularly proper to the form of God. Yet he was not haughty in that form; he did not please himself [Rom 15:3]; nor did he disdain and despise those who were enslaved and subjected to various evils.

He was not like the Pharisee who said, "God, I thank thee that I am not like other men" [Luke 18:11], for that man was delighted that others were wretched; at any rate he was unwilling that they should be like him. This is the type of robbery by which a man usurps things for himself—rather, he keeps what he has and does not clearly ascribe to God the things that are God's, nor does he serve others with them that he may become like other men. Men of this kind wish to be like God, sufficient in themselves, pleasing themselves, glorying in themselves, under obligation to no-one, and so on. Not thus, however, did Christ think; not of this stamp was his wisdom. He relinquished that form to God the Father and emptied himself, unwilling to use his rank against us, unwilling to be different from us. Moreover, for our sakes he became as one of us and took the form of a servant, that is, he subjected himself to all evils. And although he was free, as the Apostle says of himself also [1 Cor 9:19], he made himself servant of all [Mark 9:35], living as if all the evils which were ours were actually his own.

Accordingly he took upon himself our sin and our punishment, and although it was for us that he was conquering those things, he acted as though he were conquering them for himself. Although as far as his relationship to us was concerned, he had the power to be our God and Lord, yet he did not will it so, but rather desired to become our servant, as it is written in Rom 15 [:1, 3]: "We ... ought ... not to please ourselves ... For Christ did not please himself; but, as it is written, 'The reproaches of those who reproached thee fell on me'" [Ps 69:9]. The quotation from the Psalmist has the same meaning as the citation from Paul.

It follows that this passage, which many have understood affirmatively, ought to be understood negatively as follows: That Christ did not count himself equal to God means that he did not wish to be equal to him as those do who presumptuously grasp for equality and say to God, "If thou wilt not give me thy glory (as St Bernard says), I shall seize it for myself". The passage is not to be understood affirmatively as follows: He did not think himself equal to God, that is, the fact that he is equal to God, this he did not consider robbery. For this interpretation is not based on a proper understanding since it speaks of Christ the man. The Apostle means that each individual Christian shall become the servant of another in accordance with the example of Christ. If one has wisdom, righteousness, or power with which one can excel others and boast in the "form of God", so to speak, one should not keep all this to himself, but surrender it to God and become altogether as if he did not possess it [2 Cor 6:10], as one of those who lack it.

Paul's meaning is that when each person has forgotten himself and emptied himself of God's gifts, he should conduct himself as if his neighbour's weakness, sin, and foolishness were his very own. He should not boast or get puffed up. Nor should he despise or triumph over his neighbour as if he were his god or equal to God. Since God's prerogatives ought to be left to God alone, it becomes robbery when a man in haughty foolhardiness ignores this fact. It is in this way, then, that one takes the form of a servant, and that command of the Apostle in Gal 5 [:13] is fulfilled: "Through love be servants of one another". Through the figure of the members of the body Paul teaches in Rom 12 [:4-5] and 1 Cor 12 [:12-27] how the strong, honourable, healthy members do not glory over those that are weak, less honourable, and sick as if they were their masters and gods; but on the contrary they serve them the more, forgetting their own honour, health, and power. For thus no member of the body serves itself; nor does it seek its own welfare but that of the other. And the weaker, the sicker, the less honourable a member is, the more the other members serve it "that there may be no discord in the body, but that the members may have the same care for one another", to use Paul's words [1 Cor 12:25]. From this it is now evident how one must conduct himself with his neighbour in each situation.

And if we do not freely desire to put off that form of God and take on the form of a servant, let us be compelled to do so against our will. In this regard consider the story in Luke 7 [:36-50], where Simon the leper, pretending to be in the form of God and perching on his own righteousness, was arrogantly judging and despising Mary Magdalene, seeing in her the form of a servant. But see how Christ immediately stripped him of that form of righteousness and then clothed him with the form of sin by saying: "You gave me no kiss ... You did not anoint my head". How great were the sins that Simon did not see! Nor did he think himself disfigured by such a loathsome form as he had. His good works are not at all remembered.

Christ ignores the form of God in which Simon was

superciliously pleasing himself; he does not recount that he was invited, dined, and honoured by him. Simon the leper is now nothing but a sinner. He who seemed to himself so righteous sits divested of the glory of the form of God, humiliated in the form of a servant, willy-nilly. On the other hand, Christ honours Mary with the form of God and elevates her above Simon, saying: "She has anointed my feet and kissed them. She has wet my feet with her tears and wiped them with her hair". How great were the merits which neither she nor Simon saw. Her faults are remembered no more. Christ ignored the form of servitude in her whom he has exalted with the form of sovereignty. Mary is nothing but righteous, elevated into the glory of the form of God, etc.

In like manner he will treat all of us whenever we, on the ground of our righteousness, wisdom, or power, are haughty or angry with those who are unrighteous, foolish, or less powerful than we. For when we act thus—and this is the greatest perversion—righteousness works against righteousness, wisdom against wisdom, power against power. For you are powerful, not that you may make the weak weaker by oppression, but that you may make them powerful by raising them up and defending them. You are wise, not in order to laugh at the foolish and thereby make them more foolish, but that you may undertake to teach them as you yourself would wish to be taught. You are righteous that you may vindicate and pardon the unrighteous, not that you may only condemn, disparage, judge, and punish. For this is Christ's example for us, as he says: "For God sent the Son into the world, not to condemn the world, but that the world might be saved through him" [John 3:17]. He further says in Luke 9 [:55-56]: "You do not know what manner of spirit you are of; for the Son of man came not to destroy men's lives but to save them".

But the carnal nature of man violently rebels, for it greatly delights in punishment, in boasting of its own righteousness, and in its neighbour's shame and embarrassment at his unrighteousness. Therefore it pleads its own case, and it rejoices that this is better than its neighbour's. But it opposes the case of its neighbour and wants it to appear mean. This perversity is wholly evil, contrary to love, which does not seek its own good, but that of another [1 Cor 13:5; Phil 2:4]. It ought to be distressed that the condition of its neighbour is not better than its own. It ought to wish that its neighbour's condition were better than its own, and if its neighbour's condition is the better, it ought to rejoice no less than it rejoices when its own is the better. "For this is the law and the prophets" [Matt 7:12].

But you say, "Is it not permissible to chasten evil man? Is it not proper to punish sin? Who is not obliged to defend righteousness? To do otherwise would give occasion for lawlessness."

I answer: A single solution to this problem cannot be given. Therefore one must distinguish among men. For men can be classified either as public or private individuals.

The things which have been said do not pertain at all to public individuals, that is, to those who have been placed in a responsible office by God. It is their necessary function to punish and judge evil men, to vindicate and defend the oppressed, because it is not they but God who does this. They are his servants in this very matter, as the Apostle shows at some length in Rom 13 [:4]: "He does not bear the sword in vain", etc. But this must be understood as pertaining to the cases of other men, not to one's own. For no man acts in God's place for the sake of himself and his own things, but for the sake of others. If, however, a public official has a case of his own, let him ask for someone other than himself to be God's representative, for in that case he is not a judge, but one of the parties. But on these matters let others speak at other times, for it is too broad a subject to cover now.

Private individuals with their own cases are of three kinds. First, there are those who seek vengeance and judgement from the representatives of God, and of these there is now a very great number. Paul tolerates such people, but he does not approve of them when he says in 1 Cor 6 [:12], "'All things are lawful for me', but not all things are helpful". Rather he says in the same chapter, "To have lawsuits at all with one another is defeat for you" [1 Cor 6:7]. But yet to avoid a greater evil he tolerates this lesser one lest they should vindicate themselves and one should use force on the other, returning evil for evil, demanding their own advantages. Nevertheless such will not enter the kingdom of heaven unless they have changed for the better by forsaking things that are merely lawful and pursuing those that are helpful. For that passion for one's own advantage must be destroyed.

In the second class are those who do not desire vengeance. On the other hand, in accordance with the Gospel [Matt 5:40], to those who would take their coats, they are prepared to give their cloaks as well, and they do not resist any evil. These are sons of God, brothers of Christ, heirs of future blessings. In Scripture therefore they are called "fatherless", "widows", "desolate"; because they do not avenge themselves, God wishes to be called their "Father" and "Judge" [Ps 68:5]. Far from avenging themselves, if those in authority should wish to seek revenge on their behalf, they either do not desire it or seek it, or they only permit it. Or, if they are among the most advanced, they forbid and prevent it, prepared rather to lose their other possessions also.

Suppose you say: "Such people are very rare, and who would be able to remain in this world were he to do this?" I answer: This is not a discovery of today, that few are saved and that the gate is narrow that leads to life and those who find it are few [Matt 7:14]. But if none were doing this, how would the Scripture stand which calls the poor, the orphans, and the widows "the people of Christ"? Therefore those in this second class grieve more over the sin of their offenders than over the loss or offence to themselves. And they do this that they may recall those offenders from their sin rather than avenge the wrongs they themselves have suffered. Therefore they put off the form of their own righteousness and put on the form of those others, praying for their persecutors, blessing those who curse, doing good to evil-doers, prepared to pay the penalty and make satisfaction for their very enemies that they may be saved [Matt 5:44]. This is the gospel and the example of Christ [Luke 23:34].

In the third class are those who in persuasion are like the second type just mentioned, but are not like them in practice. They are the ones who demand back their own property or seek punishment to be meted out, not because they seek their own advantage, but through the punishment and restoration of their own things they seek the betterment of the one who has stolen or offended. They discern that the offender cannot be improved without punishment. These are called "zealots" and the Scriptures praise them. But no-one ought to attempt this unless he is mature and highly experienced in the second class just mentioned, lest he mistake wrath for zeal and be convicted of doing from anger and impatience that which he believes he is doing from love of justice. For anger is like zeal, and impatience is like love of justice so that they cannot be sufficiently distinguished except by the most spiritual. Christ exhibited such zeal when he made a whip and cast out the sellers and buyers from the temple, as related in John 2 [:14-17]. Paul did likewise when he said, "Shall I come to you with a rod, or with love in a spirit of gentleness?" [1 Cor 4:21].

CALVIN ON PRAYER

ow should we pray? Does God listen? What should my state of mind be when I pray, and does it make a difference?

In words written nearly five hundred years ago by John Calvin, the great Reformer of Geneva, we find answers to these age-old questions. Calvin thought very deeply about prayer. Coming from the medieval background in which it was widely believed that God could not be approached directly in prayer, Calvin was overwhelmed by the grace of God described in the Bible. His gratitude to God, and his great sense of privilege in being allowed to approach God and call him Father, flows through his writing and to us today.

The material in this 'Calvin on prayer' is taken from Calvin's *Institutes of the Christian Religion*, one of the greatest expositions of biblical doctrine in Christian history. Book I is 'The Knowledge of God the Creator', and covers how we know God, and a theology of Scripture and nature. Book II is 'The Knowledge of God the Redeemer in Christ', and explains sin and the need for redemption, and Christ as redeemer. Book III, 'The Way in Which we Receive the Grace of Christ', turns to how we take hold of Christ's work by faith, and the benefits that flow from trusting him. 'Prayer, which is the chief exercise of faith, and by which we daily receive God's benefits', is chapter 20 of Book III, and is recognized as one of the best studies of Christian prayer ever written.

The text is based on the 1960 Westminster Press edition, translated by Ford Lewis Battles. Many of its footnotes and annotations have been removed, as they make the text more difficult to read and are of real interest only to specialist scholars. The sections that refute at length the Roman Catholic doctrine of praying to saints have also been omitted.

Prayer, which is the chief exercise of faith, and by which we daily receive God's benefits

(The nature and value of prayer)
by John Calvin

Faith and prayer

From those matters so far discussed,[3] we clearly see how destitute and devoid of all good things man is, and how he lacks all aids to salvation. Therefore, if he seeks resources to help him in his need, he must go outside himself and get them elsewhere. It was afterward explained to us that the Lord willingly and freely reveals himself in his Christ. For in Christ he offers all happiness in place of our misery, all wealth in place of our neediness; in him he opens to us the heavenly treasures, that our whole faith may contemplate his beloved Son, our whole expectation depend upon him, and our whole hope cleave to and rest in him. This, indeed, is that secret and hidden philosophy which cannot be wrested from worldly logic. But they whose eyes God has opened surely learn it by heart, that in his light they may see light [Ps 36:9].

---

3.   Previous to this in *The Institutes*, Calvin has discussed justification by faith and the impossibility of salvation by works.

We have been instructed by faith to recognize that whatever we need and whatever we lack is in God, and in our Lord Jesus Christ, in whom the Father willed all the fullness of his bounty to abide so that we may all draw from it as from an overflowing spring. It remains for us to seek in him, and in prayers to ask of him, what we have learned to be in him. Otherwise, to know God as the master and bestower of all good things, who invites us to request them of him, and still not go to him and not ask of him—this would be of as little profit as for a man to neglect a treasure, buried and hidden in the earth, after it had been pointed out to him. Accordingly, the apostle, in order to show that true faith cannot be indifferent about calling upon God, has laid down this order: just as faith is born from the gospel, so through it our hearts are trained to call upon God's name [Rom 10:14-17]. And this is precisely what he had said a little before: the Spirit of adoption, who seals the witness of the gospel in our hearts, raises up our spirits to dare show forth to God their desires, to stir up unspeakable groanings [Rom 8:26], and confidently cry, "Abba! Father!" [Rom 8:15].

Now we must more fully discuss this last point, since it was previously only mentioned in passing and, as it were, briefly touched upon.

The necessity of prayer
It is, therefore, by the benefit of prayer that we reach those riches which are laid up for us with the Heavenly Father. For there is a communion of men with God by which, having entered the heavenly sanctuary, they appeal to him in person concerning his promises in order to experience, where necessity so demands, that what they believed was not vain, although he had promised it in word alone. Therefore we see

that to us nothing is promised to be expected from the Lord, which we are not also bidden to ask of him in prayers. We dig up by prayer the treasures that were pointed out by the Lord's gospel, and which our faith has gazed upon.

Words fail to explain how necessary prayer is, and in how many ways the exercise of prayer is profitable. Surely, with good reason the Heavenly Father affirms that the only stronghold of safety is in calling upon his name. By so doing we invoke the presence both of his providence, through which he watches over and guards our affairs; and of his power, through which he sustains us, weak as we are and well-nigh overcome; and of his goodness, through which he receives us, miserably burdened with sins, unto grace. In short, it is by prayer that we call him to reveal himself as wholly present to us. Hence comes an extraordinary peace and repose to our consciences. For having disclosed to the Lord the necessity that was pressing upon us, we even rest fully in the thought that none of our ills is hid from him. He, we are convinced, has both the will and the power to take the best care of us.

Objection: Is prayer not superfluous? Six reasons for it
But someone will say: does God not know, even without being reminded, both in what respect we are troubled and what is best for us, so that it may seem in a sense superfluous that he should be stirred up by our prayers—as if he were drowsily blinking or even sleeping until he is aroused by our voice? But they who think this way do not observe to what end the Lord instructed his people to pray, for he ordained it not so much for his own sake as for ours. Now he wills—as is right—that his due be rendered to him, in the recognition that everything men desire and consider beneficial comes from him, and in the declaration of this by

prayers. But the profit of this sacrifice also, by which he is worshipped, returns to us. Accordingly, the holy fathers, the more confidently they extolled God's benefits among themselves and others, were the more keenly aroused to pray. It will be enough for us to note the single example of Elijah, who, sure of God's purpose, after he has deliberately promised rain to King Ahab, still anxiously prays with his head between his knees, and sends his servant seven times to look [1 Kgs 18:42], not because he would discredit his prophecy, but because he knew it was his duty, lest his faith be sleepy or sluggish, to lay his desires before God.

Therefore, even though, while we grow dull and stupid toward our miseries, he watches and keeps guard on our behalf, and sometimes even helps us unasked, still it is very important for us to call upon him. First, so that our hearts may be fired with a zealous and burning desire ever to seek, love, and serve him, while we become accustomed in every need to flee to him as to a sacred anchor. Secondly, that there may enter our hearts no desire and no wish at all of which we should be ashamed to make him a witness, while we learn to set all our wishes before his eyes, and even to pour out our whole hearts. Thirdly, that we be prepared to receive his benefits with true gratitude of heart and thanksgiving, benefits that our prayer reminds us come from his hand. Fourthly, moreover, that having obtained what we were seeking, and being convinced that he has answered our prayers, we should be led to meditate upon his kindness more ardently. And fifthly, that at the same time we embrace with greater delight those things which we acknowledge to have been obtained by prayers. Finally, that use and experience may, according to the measure of our feebleness, confirm his providence. Thus we will understand not only that he promises never to fail us, and of his own will opens the way to call upon him at the very point of necessity, but also that he ever extends his hand to help his own, not wet-nursing them with words but defending them with present help.

On account of these things, our most merciful Father, although he never either sleeps or idles, still very often gives the impression of one sleeping or idling in order that he may thus train us—otherwise idle and lazy—to seek, ask, and entreat him to our great good.

Therefore people act with excessive foolishness when, to call men's minds away from prayer, they babble that God's providence, standing guard over all things, is vainly called upon with our entreaties. For, on the contrary, the Lord has not 'vainly' attested that "he is near ... to all who call upon his name in truth" [Ps 145:18]. Quite like this is what others go on with: that it is quite unnecessary for them to petition for things that the Lord is gladly ready to bestow. In fact, those very things which flow to us from his voluntary generosity he would have us recognize as granted to our prayers. That memorable saying of the psalm attests this, and to it many similar passages correspond: "For the eyes of the Lord are upon the righteous, and his ears toward their prayers" [Ps 34:15]. This sentence so commends the providence of God—intent of his own accord upon caring for the salvation of the godly—as yet not to omit the exercise of faith, by which men's minds are cleansed of laziness. The eyes of God are therefore watchful to assist the blind in their necessity, but he is willing in turn to hear our groanings that he may the better prove his love toward us. And so both are true: "that the keeper of Israel neither slumbers nor sleeps" [Ps 121:4], and yet that he is inactive, as if forgetting us, when he sees us idle and mute.

The rules of right prayer
First rule: reverence

Devout detachment required for conversation with God

Now for framing prayer duly and properly, let this be the first rule: that we be disposed in mind and heart as befits those who enter conversation with God. This we shall indeed attain with respect to the mind if it is freed from carnal cares and thoughts which lead it away from right and pure contemplation of God, and then not only devotes itself completely to prayer but also, in so far as this is possible, is lifted and carried beyond itself. Now I do not here require the mind to be so detached as never to be pricked or gnawed by vexations, since, on the contrary, great anxiety should kindle in us the desire to pray. Thus we see that God's saintly servants give proof of huge torments, not to say vexations, when they speak of uttering their plaintive cry to the Lord from the deep abyss, and from the very jaws of death. But I say that we are to rid ourselves of all alien and outside cares, by which the mind, itself a wanderer, is borne about hither and thither, drawn away from heaven, and pressed down to earth. I mean that it ought to be raised above itself that it may not bring into God's sight anything our blind and stupid reason likes to devise, nor hold itself within the limits of its own vanity, but rise to a purity worthy of God.

Against undisciplined and irreverent prayer

These two matters are well worth attention: first, whoever engages in prayer should apply to it his faculties and efforts, and not, as commonly happens, be distracted by wandering thoughts. For nothing is more contrary to reverence for God than the levity that marks an excess of frivolity utterly devoid of awe. In this matter, the harder we find concentration to be, the more strenuously we ought to labour after it. For no-one is so intent on praying that he does not feel many irrelevant thoughts stealing upon him, which either break the course of prayer or delay it by some winding bypath. But here let us recall how unworthy it is, when God admits us to intimate conversation, to abuse his great kindness by mixing sacred and profane; but just as if the discourse were between us and an ordinary man, amidst our prayers we neglect him and flit about hither and thither.

Let us therefore realize that the only persons who duly and properly gird themselves to pray are those who are so moved by God's majesty that they come to it freed from earthly cares and affections. And the rite of raising the hands means that men remember they are far removed from God unless they raise their thoughts on high. As it is also said in the psalm: "To you ... I have lifted up my soul" [Ps 25:1]. And Scripture quite often uses this expression, "to lift up prayer", in order that those who wish God to hear them may not settle down "on their dregs" [cf. Jer 48:11]. In short, the more generously God deals with us, gently summoning us to unburden our cares into his bosom, the less excusable are we if his splendid and incomparable benefit does not outweigh all else with us and draw us to him, so that we apply our minds and efforts zealously to prayer. This cannot happen unless the mind, stoutly wrestling with these hindrances, rises above them.

We have noted another point: not to ask any more than God allows. For even though he bids us pour out our hearts before him, he still does not indiscriminately slacken the reins to stupid and wicked emotions; and while he promises that he will act according to the will of the godly, his gentleness does not go so far that he yields to their wilfulness. Yet in both, men commonly sin gravely; for many rashly, shamelessly, and irreverently dare importune God with their improprieties and impudently present before his throne whatever in dreams has struck their fancy. But such great dullness or stupidity grips them that they dare thrust upon God all their vilest desires, which they would be deeply ashamed to acknowledge to men. Certain profane authors made fun of and even detested this effrontery, but the vice itself has always held sway; and hence it came to pass that ambitious men chose Jupiter as their patron; the miserly, Mercury; those greedy for knowledge, Apollo and Minerva; the warlike, Mars; the lecherous, Venus. Even so today, as I have just suggested, men in their prayers grant more license to their unlawful desires than if equals were jestingly to gossip with equals. Yet, God does not allow his gentle dealing to be thus mocked but, claiming his own right, he subjects our wishes to his power and bridles them. For this reason, we must hold fast to John's statement: "This is the confidence we have in him, that if we ask anything according to his will, he hears us" [1 John 5:14].

The Holy Spirit aids right prayer

But because our abilities are far from able to match such perfection, we must seek a remedy to help us. As we must turn keenness of mind toward God, so affection of heart has to follow. Both, indeed, stand far beneath; nay, more truly, they faint and fail, or are carried in the opposite direction. Therefore, in order to minister to this weakness, God gives us the Spirit as our teacher in prayer, to tell us what is right and temper our emotions. For, "because we do not know how to pray as we ought, the Spirit comes to our help" and "intercedes for us with unspeakable groans" [Rom 8:26]; not that he actually prays or groans but arouses in us assurance, desires, and sighs, which our natural powers would scarcely be able to conceive. And Paul, with good reason, calls "unspeakable" these groans which believers give forth under the guidance of the Spirit; for they who are truly trained in prayers are not unmindful that, perplexed by blind anxieties, they are so constrained as scarcely to know what it is worthwhile for them to utter. Indeed, when they try to stammer, they are confused and hesitate. Clearly, then, to pray rightly is a rare gift. These things are not said in order that we, favouring our own slothfulness, may give over the function of prayer to the Spirit of God, and vegetate in that carelessness to which we are all too prone. In this strain we hear the impious voices of certain persons, saying that we should drowsily wait until he overtake our preoccupied minds. But rather our intention is that, loathing our inertia and dullness, we should seek such aid of the Spirit. And indeed, Paul, when he enjoins us to pray in the Spirit, does not stop urging us to watchfulness. He means that the prompting of the Spirit empowers us so to compose prayers as by no means to hinder or hold back our own effort, since in this matter God's will is to test how effectually faith moves our hearts.

Second rule: we pray from a sincere sense of want, and with penitence

The sense of need that excludes all unreality

Let this be the second rule: that in our petitions we ever sense our own insufficiency, and earnestly pondering how we need all that we seek, join with this prayer an earnest—nay, burning—desire to attain it. For many perfunctorily intone prayers after a set form, as if discharging a duty to God. And although they admit it to be a necessary remedy for their ills, because it would be fatal to lack the help of God which they are beseeching, still it appears that they perform this duty from habit, because their hearts are meanwhile cold, and they do not ponder what they ask. Indeed, a general and confused feeling of their need leads them to prayer, but it does not arouse them, as it were in present reality, to seek the relief of their poverty. Now what do we account more hateful or even execrable to God than the fiction of someone asking pardon for his sins, all the while either thinking he is not a sinner or at least not thinking he is a sinner? Unquestionably something in which God himself is mocked! Yet, as I have just said, mankind is so stuffed with such depravity that for the sake of mere performance men often beseech God for many things that they are dead sure will, apart from his kindness, come to them from some other source, or already lie in their possession.

A fault that seems less serious but is also not tolerable is that of others who, having been imbued with this one principle—that God must be appeased by devotions—mumble prayers without meditation. Now the godly must particularly beware of presenting themselves before God to request anything unless they yearn for it with sincere affection of heart, and at the same time desire to obtain it from him. Indeed, even though those things which we seek only to God's glory do not seem at first glance to be for our own need, yet it is fitting that they be sought with no less ardour and eagerness. When, for example, we pray that "his name be sanctified" [Matt 6:9; Luke 11:2], we should, so to speak, eagerly hunger and thirst after that sanctification.

Is prayer at times dependent upon our passing mood?
If anyone should object that we are not always urged with equal necessity to pray, I admit it. And to our benefit James

gives us this distinction: "Is anyone among you sad? Let him pray. Is any cheerful? Let him sing" [Jas 5:13]. Therefore common sense itself dictates that, because we are too lazy, God pricks us the more sharply, as occasion demands, to pray earnestly. David calls this a "seasonable time" [Ps 32:6] because, as he teaches in many other passages, the more harshly troubles, discomforts, fears, and trials of other sorts press us, the freer is our access to him, as if God were summoning us to himself.

At the same time Paul's statement is no less true, that we must "pray at all times" [1 Thess 5:17]. For however much after our heart's desire affairs may prosperously flow and occasion for happiness surround us on all sides, still there is no point of time when our need does not urge us to pray. A certain man has abundant wine and grain. Since he cannot enjoy a single morsel of bread apart from God's continuing favour, his wine cellars and granaries will not hinder him from praying for his daily bread. Now if we should consider how many dangers at every moment threaten, fear itself will teach us that we at no single time may leave off praying.

Still, we can better recognize this fact in spiritual matters. For when should the many sins of which we are conscious allow us nonchalantly to stop praying as suppliants for pardon of our guilt and penalty? When do temptations yield us a truce from hastening after help? Moreover, zeal for the Kingdom of God and his glory ought so to lay hold on us, not intermittently but constantly, that the same opportunity may ever remain ours. It is therefore not in vain that constancy in prayer is enjoined upon us. I am not yet speaking of perseverance, of which mention will be made later; but Scripture, admonishing us to "pray constantly", accuses us of sloth, for we do not realize how much we need this attentiveness and constancy. By this rule, hypocrisy and wily falsehoods toward God are debarred from prayer—indeed, are banished far away! God promises that "he will be near to all who call upon him in truth" [Ps 145:18], and states that those who seek him with all their heart will find him [Jer 29:13-14]. For this reason, they who delight in their own foulness aspire not at all. Lawful prayer, therefore, demands repentance. Hence arises the common thought in Scripture that God does not hearken to the wicked, and that their prayers—like their sacrifices—are abominable to him. For it is right that they who bar their hearts should find God's ears closed, and that they who by their hardheartedness provoke his severity should not feel him conciliatory. In Isaiah he threatens in this way: "Even though you multiply your prayers, I will not listen; for your hands are full of blood" [Isa 1:15]. Again, in Jeremiah: "I cried out ... and they refused to listen; ... they will cry out in return, and I will not listen" [Jer 11:7, 8, 11]. For he counts it the height of dishonour for wicked men, who all their lives besmirch his sacred name, to boast of his covenant. Consequently, in Isaiah he complains, when the Jews "draw near to him with their lips ... their hearts are far from him" [Isa 29:13]. He does not, indeed, restrict this to prayers alone but declares that falsity in any part of his worship is abhorrent to him. That statement of James applies here. "You seek, and do not receive because you ask wrongly to spend it on your passions" [Jas 4:3]. It is indeed true, as we shall again see a little later, that the prayers poured out by the godly do not depend upon their worthiness; yet John's warning is not superfluous: "We receive from him whatever we ask because we keep his commandments" [1 John 3:22], while a bad conscience closes the door to us. From this it follows that only sincere worshippers of God pray aright and are heard. Let each one, therefore, as he prepares to pray be displeased with his own evil deeds; and (something that cannot happen without repentance) let him take the person and disposition of a beggar.

Third rule: we yield all confidence in ourselves and humbly plead for pardon

We come as humble suppliants for mercy

To this let us join a third rule: let anyone who stands before God to pray, in his humility giving glory completely to God, abandon all thought of his own glory, cast off all notion of his own worth, in sum, put away all self-assurance—lest if we claim for ourselves anything, even the least bit, we should become vainly puffed up, and perish at his presence. We have repeated examples of this humble submission in God's servants; each one of whom, the holier he is, the more he is cast down when he presents himself before the Lord. Thus spoke Daniel, whom the Lord himself commended with so great a title: "We do not pour forth our prayers to you on the ground of our righteousnesses but on the ground of your great mercy. O Lord, hear us; O Lord, be kind to us. Hear us, and do what we ask ... for your own sake ... because your name is called upon over your people, and over your holy place" [Dan 9:18-19]. Nor does he, by a devious figure of speech, as some men do, mingle with the crowd as one of the people. Rather he confesses his guilt as an individual, and as a beggar takes refuge in God's pardon, as he eloquently declares: "When I had ... confessed my sin and the sin of my people" [Dan 9:20]. David also urges this humility by his own example: "Enter not into judgement with your servant, for no man living is righteous before you" [Ps 143:2]. In such a form, Isaiah prays: "Behold, you were angry, for we sinned ...

The world is founded upon your ways, therefore we shall be saved ... And all of us have been full of uncleanness, and all our righteousnesses like a filthy rag; we all have faded like a leaf, and our iniquities, like the wind, scatter us. There is no-one who calls upon your name, who bestirs himself to take hold of you. For you have hidden your face from us, and have made us to melt away in the hand of our iniquities. Yet, O Lord, you are our Father; we are the clay, you are our potter and we are the work of your hand. Be not angry, O Lord, and remember not iniquity forever. Behold now, consider, we are all your people" [Isa 64:5-9].

Observe that they depend on no assurance whatever but this alone: that, reckoning themselves to be of God, they do not despair that he will take care of them. Likewise, Jeremiah: "Though our sins testify against us, act ... for your name's sake" [Jer 14:7]. For some unknown author, whoever he may be, has written these very true and holy words attributed to the prophet Baruch:[4] "The soul that is sorrowful and desolate for the greatness of her evil, bowed down and feeble ... the hungry soul, and the eyes that fail give glory ... to you, O Lord. It is not for the righteousnesses of the fathers that we pour out our prayers before you, and beg mercy in your sight, O Lord our God"; but because you are merciful, "be merciful unto us, for we have sinned before you" [Baruch 3:2].

The plea for forgiveness of sins as the most important part of prayer
To sum up: the beginning, and even the preparation, of proper prayer is the plea for pardon with a humble and sincere confession of guilt. Nor should anyone, however holy he may

4. Baruch was Jeremiah's scribe (see Jer 36:4); the apocryphal 'Book of Baruch' is attributed to him.

be, hope that he will obtain anything from God until he is freely reconciled to him; nor can God chance to be favourable to any but those whom he has pardoned. Accordingly, it is no wonder if believers open for themselves the door to prayer with this key, as we learn from numerous passages of the Psalms. For David, asking for something else than remission of his sins, says: "Remember not the sins of my youth, and my transgressions; according to your mercy remember me, for your goodness' sake, O Lord" [Ps 25:7]. Again: "See my affliction and my toil, and forgive all my sins" [Ps 25:18].

Also, in this we see that it is not enough for us to call ourselves to account each day for recent sins if we do not remember those sins which might seem to have been long forgotten. For the same prophet, elsewhere having confessed one grave offence, on this occasion even turns back to his mother's womb, in which he had contracted the infection, not to extenuate the guilt on the ground of corruption of nature but that, in gathering up the sins of his whole life, the more rigorously he condemns himself, the more easily entreated he may find God. But even though the saints do not always beg forgiveness of sins in so many words, if we diligently ponder their prayers that Scripture relates, we shall readily come upon what I speak of: that they have received their intention to pray from God's mercy alone, and thus always have begun with appeasing him. For if anyone should question his own conscience, he would be so far from daring intimately to lay aside his cares before God that, unless he relied upon mercy and pardon, he would tremble at every approach.

There is also another special confession when suppliants ask release from punishments. It is that at the same time they may pray for the pardon of their sins. For it would be absurd to wish the effect to be removed while the cause remained. We must guard against imitating foolish sick folk, who, concerned solely with the treatment of symptoms, neglect the very root of the disease. We must make it our first concern that God be favourable toward us, rather than that he attest his favour by outward signs. He wills to maintain this order, and it would have been of small profit to us to have him do us good unless our conscience, feeling him wholly appeased, rendered him altogether lovely. Christ's reply also reminds us of this; for after he had decided to heal the paralytic, he said "Your sins are forgiven you" [Matt 9:2]. He thus arouses our minds to that which we ought especially to desire: that God may receive us into grace; then, that in aiding us he may set forth the fruit of reconciliation.

But besides that special confession of present guilt, with which believers plead for the remission of every sin and penalty, the general preface that gains favour for prayers must never be passed over, for unless they are founded in free mercy, prayers never reach God. John's statement can be applied to this: "If we confess our sins, he is faithful and just to forgive ... and cleanse us from all unrighteousness" [1 John 1:9]. For this reason, under the law prayers had to be consecrated with blood atonement in order that they should be accepted, and that the people should thus be warned that they were unworthy of so great a privilege of honour until, purged of their defilement, they derived confidence in prayer solely from God's mercy.

Reference to one's own righteousness?
Now, the saints sometimes seem to shout approval of their own righteousness in calling upon God for help. For example, David says: "Keep my life, for I am good" [Ps 86:2]; and

similarly, Hezekiah: "Remember ... O Lord, I beseech you, how I have walked before you in truth ... and have done what is good in your sight" [2 Kgs 20:3]. By such expressions they mean nothing else but that by their regeneration itself they are attested as servants and children of God to whom he promises that he will be gracious. He teaches through the prophet, as we have already seen, that his eyes "are upon the righteous, his ears toward their prayers" [Ps 34:15]. Again, through the apostle John: "We shall receive ... whatever we ask if we keep his commandments" [1 John 3:22]. In these statements he does not set the value of prayer according to the merits of works, but he is pleased to establish the assurance of those who are duly aware of uprightness and innocence, as all believers ought to be. Indeed, what the blind man whose sight was restored says in John's gospel—that God does not listen to sinners [John 9:31]—has been drawn from the very truth of God, provided we understand "sinners" in the customary usage of Scripture, as all persons who slumber and repose in their own sins without any desire for righteousness. For no heart can ever break into sincere calling upon God that does not at the same time aspire to godliness. The saints' claims to righteousness depend upon such promises. They mention their purity or innocence simply that they may show the reality of that godliness which all God's servants should hope for.

Again, while they are before the Lord comparing themselves with their enemies, from whose iniquity they long to be delivered by his hand, they are commonly found using this sort of prayer. Now it is no wonder if in this comparison they put forward their own righteousness and simplicity of heart in order that, from the equity of the cause itself, they might move the Lord to provide them with assistance. The godly man enjoys a pure conscience before the Lord, thus confirming himself in the promises with which the Lord comforts and supports his true worshippers. It is not our intent to snatch this blessing from his breast; rather, we would assert that the assurance his prayers will be answered rests solely upon God's grace, apart from all consideration of personal merit.

Fourth rule: we pray with confident hope
Hope and faith overcome fear

The fourth rule is that, thus cast down and overcome by true humility, we should be nonetheless encouraged to pray by a sure hope that our prayer will be answered. These are indeed things apparently contrary: to join the firm assurance of God's favour to a sense of his just vengeance; yet, on the ground that God's goodness alone raises up those oppressed by their own evil deeds, they very well agree together. For, in accordance with our previous teaching that repentance and faith are companions joined together by an indissoluble bond, although one of these terrifies us while the other gladdens us, so also these two ought to be present together in prayers. And David briefly expresses this agreement when he says: "Through the abundance of your goodness I will enter your house; I will worship toward your holy temple with fear" [Ps 5:7]. Under God's goodness he includes faith, meantime not excluding fear. For not only does his majesty constrain us to reverence but through our own unworthiness, forgetting all pride and self-confidence, we are held in fear.

But I do not understand "assurance" to mean that which soothes our mind with sweet and perfect repose, releasing it from every anxiety. For to repose so peacefully is the attitude of those who, when all affairs are flowing to their liking, are touched by no care, burn with no desire, toss with no fear. But for the saints the occasion that best stimulates them to call upon God is when, distressed by their own need, they are troubled by the greatest unrest, and are almost driven out of their senses, until faith opportunely comes to their relief. For among such tribulations God's goodness so shines upon them that even when they groan with weariness under the weight of present ills, and also are troubled and tormented by the fear of greater ones, yet, relying upon his goodness, they are relieved of the difficulty of bearing them, and are comforted and hope for escape and deliverance. It is fitting therefore that the godly man's prayer arise from these two emotions, and that it also contain and represent both. That is, that he groan under present ills and anxiously fear those to come, yet at the same time take refuge in God, not at all doubting he is ready to extend his helping hand. It is amazing how much our lack of trust provokes God if we request of him a blessing that we do not expect.

Prayer and faith
Therefore nothing is more in harmony with the nature of prayers than that this rule be laid down and established for them: that they not break forth by chance but follow faith as guide. Christ calls this principle to the attention of all of us with this saying: "I say to you, whatever you seek ... believe that you will receive it, and it will come to you" [Mark 11:24]. He confirms the same statement in another place: "Whatever you ask in prayer, believing ..." etc. [Matt 21:22]. James is in accord with this: "If any of you lack wisdom, let him ask God, who gives to all men simply and without reproaching ... Let him ask in faith, with no wavering" [Jas 1:5-6]. There, opposing faith to wavering, he most appropriately expresses

the force of faith. Nonetheless, what he adds must also be noted: that they who in doubt and perplexity call upon God, uncertain in their minds whether they will be heard or not, will gain nothing. He even compares these persons to waves that are driven and tossed hither and thither by the wind [Jas 1:6]. Hence, in another passage, James calls what is right and proper "the prayer of faith" [Jas 5:15]. Then, since God so often affirms that he will give to each one according to his faith, he implies that we can obtain nothing apart from faith.

To sum up, it is faith that obtains whatever is granted to prayer. Such is the meaning of Paul's famous statement, which the unwise too little regard: "How will anyone call upon him in whom he has not believed? And who will believe unless he has heard?" [Rom 10:14]. "Faith comes by hearing, and hearing from the Word of God" [Rom 10:17]. For, deducing step by step the beginning of prayer from faith, he plainly asserts that God cannot be sincerely called upon by others than those to whom, through the preaching of the gospel, his kindness and gentle dealing have become known—indeed, have been intimately revealed.

Against the denial of certainty that prayer is granted
Our opponents do not at all ponder this requirement. Therefore, when we urge believers to be convinced with firm assurance of mind that God is favourable and benevolent to them, they think we are saying the most absurd thing of all. Still, if they made any use of true prayer, they would really understand that without that firm sense of the divine benevolence God could not be rightly called upon. Since no-one can well perceive the power of faith unless he feels it by experience in his heart, what point is there in arguing with

men of this sort, who clearly show that they have never had anything but an empty imagination? For the value and need of that assurance, which we require, is chiefly learned from calling upon him. He who does not see this shows that he has a very unfeeling conscience. Let us, then, pass over this class of blind persons, and hold firmly to the statement of Paul's: God cannot be called upon by any except those who have learned of his mercy from the gospel, and have surely been persuaded that it has been prepared for them.

Now what sort of prayer will this be? "O Lord, I am in doubt whether you wish to hear me, but because I am pressed by anxiety, I flee to you, that, if I am worthy, you may help me." This is not the way of all the saints whose prayers we read in Scripture. And the Holy Spirit did not so instruct us through the apostle, who enjoins us to "draw near to the heavenly throne ... with confidence, that we may receive ... grace" [Heb 4:16]; and teaches elsewhere that we have boldness and access in confidence through faith in Christ [Eph 3:12]. If we would pray fruitfully, we ought therefore to grasp with both hands this assurance of obtaining what we ask, which the Lord enjoins with his own voice, and all the saints teach by their example. For only that prayer is acceptable to God which is born, if I may so express it, out of such presumption of faith, and is grounded in unshaken assurance of hope. He could have been content with the simple mention of faith, yet he not only added confidence but also fortified it with freedom or boldness, that by this mark he might distinguish from us the unbelievers, who indeed indiscriminately mingle with us in our prayers to God, but by chance. The whole church prays in this way in the psalm: "Let your mercy be upon us, even as we have hoped in you" [Ps 33:22]. Elsewhere the prophet lays down the same condition: "In the day when I call, this I know, that God is with me" [Ps 56:9]. Likewise: "In the morning I will make ready for you, and watch" [Ps 5:3]. From these words we conclude that prayers are vainly cast upon the air unless hope be added, from which we quietly watch for God as from a watchtower. Paul's order of exhortation agrees with these: for before he urges believers "to pray at all times in the Spirit" with watchfulness and perseverance [Eph 6:18], he bids them first take up "the shield of faith … the helmet of salvation, and the sword of the Spirit, which is the word of God" [Eph 6:16-17].

Here let my readers recall what I said before: that faith is not at all overthrown when it is joined with the acknowledgment of our misery, destitution, and uncleanness. For however much believers may feel pressed down or troubled by a heavy weight of sins—not only bereft of all things that might obtain favour with God, but laden with many offences that justly render him terrifying—nevertheless they do not cease to come before him. This feeling does not frighten them from presenting themselves to him, since there is no other access to him. For prayer was not ordained that we should be haughtily puffed up before God, or greatly esteem anything of ours, but that, having confessed our guilt, we should deplore our distresses before him, as children unburden their troubles to their parents. Moreover, the boundless mass of our sins should amply furnish us with spurs or goads to arouse us to pray, as the prophet also teaches us by his example: "Heal my soul, for I have sinned against you" [Ps 41:4]. Indeed, I confess that in these darts there would be deadly stings if God did not help us. But according to his incomparable compassion, our most gracious Father has added a timely remedy, for in calming all anxiety, easing cares, and casting out fears, he draws us gently to himself—

nay, removing all rough spots, not to mention hindrances, he paves the way.

God's command and promise as motive for prayer
First, in calling us to pray, the very command itself convicts us of impious obstinacy unless we obey. Nothing could be commanded more precisely than what is stated in the psalm: "Call upon me in the day of tribulation" [Ps 50:15]. I hardly need dwell longer on this point since the Scriptures themselves commend no duty of godliness more frequently. "Seek", says the Master, "and you will receive; knock, and it will be opened unto you" [Matt 7:7]. However, a promise is here also added to the precept, as is necessary; for even though all admit that the precept ought to be obeyed, still the majority would flee from God when he calls if he did not promise to be easily entreated and readily accessible.

When these two things have been established, it is certain that those who try to wriggle out of coming directly to God are not only rebellious and stubborn but are also convicted of unbelief because they distrust the promises. This is all the more noteworthy, since hypocrites on the pretence of humility and modesty haughtily despise God's precept and also discredit his kindly invitation—even defraud him of the chief part of his worship. For having rejected sacrifices in which all holiness then seemed to rest, he declares that to be called upon in the day of need is highest and precious above all else [Ps 50:7-15]. Therefore, when he requires what is his, and spurs us to eager obedience, there are no colours of doubt, however alluring, that can excuse us. So then, all the passages that keep occurring in the Scriptures, in which calling upon God is enjoined upon us, are as so many banners set up before our eyes to inspire us with confidence. It would be rashness itself to burst into God's sight if he himself had not anticipated our coming by calling us. Therefore he opens a way for us in his own words: "I will say to them, 'You are my people'; they will say to me, 'You are our God'" [Zech 13:9]. We see how he precedes those who worship him, and would have them follow him, and thus not to fear for the sweetness of the melody that he himself dictates.

Especially let that noble title of God come to our minds, and let us rely upon it so that we shall without trouble overcome all obstacles. "O God ... you who hear prayer! To you shall all flesh come" [Ps 65:1-2]. For what is more lovely or agreeable than for God to bear this title, which assures us that nothing is more to his nature than to assent to our prayers? From this the prophet infers that the door is open not to a few but to all mortals, for he addresses all in these words: "Call upon me in the day of affliction; I will deliver you, and you shall glorify me" [Ps 50:15]. According to this rule, David claims for himself the promise given him, that he may obtain what he seeks. "You ... O God, have revealed to the ear of your servant ... therefore your servant has found courage to pray" [2 Sam 7:27]. From this we conclude that he was fearful except in so far as the promise had encouraged him. So elsewhere he arms himself with this general doctrine: "He will do the will of those who fear him" [Ps 145:19]. Indeed, we may note this in the Psalms: that if the thread of prayer were broken, transition is sometimes made to God's power, sometimes to his goodness, sometimes to the faithfulness of his promises. It might seem that David, by inserting these statements inopportunely, mutilates his prayers, but believers know by use and experience that ardour burns low unless they supply new fuel. Accordingly, among our prayers, meditation both on God's nature and on his Word is by no means

superfluous. And so by David's example, let us not disdain
to insert something that may refresh our languishing spirits
with new vigour.

Men should pray confidently, without terror but with reverential fear

It is strange that by promises of such great sweetness we are
affected either so coldly or hardly at all, so that many of us
prefer to wander through mazes and, forsaking the fountain
of living waters, to dig out for ourselves dry cisterns [Jer
2:13], rather than to embrace God's generosity, freely given
to us. "The name of the Lord is an impregnable citadel", says
Solomon; "the righteous man will flee to it and be saved"
[Prov 18:10]. But Joel, after he has prophesied the frightful
ruin that threatens, adds this memorable sentence: "All that
call upon the name of the Lord shall be delivered" [Joel 2:32].
This we know actually refers to the course of the gospel.
Scarcely one man in a hundred is moved to approach God.
He himself proclaims through Isaiah: "You will call upon me
and I shall hear you. Nay, before you call, I will answer you"
[Isa 65:24]. Elsewhere he also gives this same honour to the
whole church in common, as it applies to all the members of
Christ. "He has called to me and I shall hearken to him; I am
with him in tribulation to rescue him" [Ps 91:15]. Still, it is
not my purpose, as I have already said, to list every passage
but to choose certain pre-eminent ones, from which we may
taste how gently God attracts us to himself, and with what
tight bonds our ungratefulness is bound when, amidst such
sharp pricks, our sluggishness still delays. Accordingly, let
these words ever resound in our ears: "The Lord is near to all
who call upon him, who call upon him in truth" [Ps 145:18].
It is the same with the words we have quoted from Isaiah and

Joel, with which God assures us that he is attentive to our prayers, and is even pleased as by a sacrifice of sweet savour when we "cast our cares upon him". We receive this singular fruit of God's promises when we frame our prayers without hesitation or fear; but, relying upon the word of him whose majesty would otherwise terrify us, we dare call upon him as Father, while he deigns to suggest this sweetest of names to us.

It remains for us, provided with such inducements, to know that we have from this enough evidence that he will hearken to us, inasmuch as our prayers depend upon no merit of ours, but their whole worth and hope of fulfilment are grounded in God's promises, and depend upon them. They need no other support, nor ought they look about up and down, hither and thither. We must therefore make up our minds that, even though we do not excel in a holiness like that which is praised in the holy patriarchs, prophets, and apostles, yet because we and they have a common command to pray and a common faith, if we rely upon God's Word, in this we are rightly their fellows. For God, as has been seen above, declaring that he will be gentle and kind to all, gives to those who are utterly miserable, hope that they will get what they have sought. Accordingly, we must note the general forms, by which no-one from first to last (as people say) is excluded, provided sincerity of heart, dissatisfaction with ourselves, humility, and faith are present in order that our hypocrisy may not profane God's name by calling upon him deceitfully. Our most gracious Father will not cast out those whom he not only urges, but stirs up with every possible means, to come to him. Hence arises David's way of praying, to which I have recently referred: "Behold, Lord, you have promised your servant ... therefore your servant has today taken heart and found what he might pray before you. And now, O Lord God, you are God, and your words will be true. You have spoken of these benefits to your servant. Now begin and do it" [2 Sam 7:27-29]. As also elsewhere: "Grant to your servant according to your word" [Ps 119:76]. And all the Israelites together, whenever they arm themselves by remembering the covenant, sufficiently assert that since God so enjoins, one is not to pray fearfully. In this they followed the examples of the patriarchs, especially Jacob, who, after he confessed himself to be less than the many mercies he had received at God's hand, says that he is nevertheless encouraged to ask greater things because God had promised that he would do them.

But whatever pretences unbelievers present, when they do not flee to God whenever necessity presses, do not seek him, and do not implore his help, they defraud him just as much of his due honour as if they made new gods and idols, since in this way they deny God is the author of every good thing. On the other hand, nothing is more effective to free the godly from every misgiving than to be fortified with this thought: there is no reason why any delay should hinder them while they obey the commandment of God, who declares that nothing pleases him more than obedience.

Hence what I have previously said is shown again in clearer light: that a dauntless spirit of praying rightly accords with fear, reverence, and concern, and it is not absurd if God raises those who lie prostrate. In this way expressions seemingly discordant beautifully agree. Jeremiah and Daniel say that they lay their prayers before God. Elsewhere Jeremiah says: "Let our supplication fall before you that the remnant of your people may be pitied" [Jer 42:2]. On the other hand, believers are often said to "lift up prayer".

So speaks Hezekiah, when he asks the prophet to intercede on his behalf. And David longs to have his prayer rise up "as incense". That is, even though because they are persuaded of God's fatherly love they gladly commit themselves to his safekeeping and do not hesitate to implore the assistance that he freely promises, still they are not elated by heedless confidence, as if they had cast away shame. They so climb upward by the steps of the promises that they still remain humble in their self-abasement.

God hearkens even to defective prayers
Hearkening to imperfect prayer

Here more than one question is raised: for Scripture relates that God has granted fulfilment of certain prayers, despite the fact that they have burst forth from a heart not at all peaceful or composed. For due cause, yet aroused by passionate wrath and vengeance, Jotham had vowed the inhabitants of Shechem to the destruction that later overtook them; God in allowing the curse seems to approve ill-controlled outbreaks. Such passion also seized Samson, when he said: "Strengthen me, O God, that I may take vengeance on the uncircumcised" [Judg 16:28]. For even though there was some righteous zeal mixed in, still a burning and hence vicious longing for vengeance was in control. God granted the petition. From this, it seems, we may infer that, although prayers are not framed to the rule of the Word, they obtain their effect.

I reply that a universal law is not disproved by individual examples; further, that special impulses have sometimes been imparted to a few men, by which it came about that a different consideration applied to them than to the common folk. For we must note Christ's answer when his disciples heedlessly desired him to emulate the example of Elijah, that they did not know with what sort of spirit they were endowed.

But we must go further: the prayers that God grants are not always pleasing to him. But in so far as example is concerned, what Scripture teaches is revealed by clear proofs: that he helps the miserable and hearkens to the groans of those who, unjustly afflicted, implore his aid; therefore, that he executes his judgements while complaints of the poor rise up to him, although they are unworthy to receive even a trifle. For how often did he, punishing the cruelty, robberies, violence, lust, and other crimes of the ungodly, silencing their boldness and rage; also overturning their tyrannical power, attest that he helps those wrongly oppressed, who yet beat the air with praying to an unknown god? And one psalm clearly teaches that prayers which do not reach heaven by faith still are not without effect. The psalm lumps together those prayers which, out of natural feeling, necessity wrings from unbelievers just as much as from believers, yet from the outcome it proves that God is gracious toward them [Ps 107:6, 13, 19]. Is it because he with such gentleness attests the prayers to be acceptable to him? Nay, it is by this circumstance to emphasize or illumine his mercy whenever the prayers of unbelievers are not denied to them; and again to incite his true worshippers to pray the more, when they see that even ungodly wailings sometimes do some good.

Yet there is no reason why believers should turn aside from a law divinely imposed upon them, or should envy unbelievers, as if from having gotten what they wished they had made great gain. We said that in this way God was moved by Ahab's feigned penitence [1 Kgs 21:29] in order to prove by this evidence how easily entreated he is toward his elect when they come with true conversion to appease him. Therefore, in Psalm 106, he blames the Jews because, having found him receptive to their pleas, they shortly after reverted to the stubbornness of their nature. This is also perfectly clear from the history of the Judges: whenever the Israelites wept, even though their tears were false, yet they were rescued from their enemies' hands. Just as God causes his sun to shine alike upon the good and the evil, so he does not despise the weeping of those whose cause is just and whose distresses deserve to be relieved. Meanwhile, in listening to the prayers of the evil, he no more grants them salvation than he supplies food to those who despise his goodness.

In the cases of Abraham and Samuel, more difficult questions seem to arise—the one, instructed by no word of God, prayed for the people of Sodom; the other prayed for Saul, even against a downright prohibition. Jeremiah acted similarly when he prayed that the destruction of the city be averted. For although they suffered a refusal, it seems hard to judge them as not having faith. But this solution, I trust, will satisfy moderate readers: relying upon the general principles by which God bids us bestow mercy even upon the unworthy, they did not utterly lack faith, although in this particular instance their opinion deceived them. Augustine somewhere wisely states: "How do the saints pray in faith when they seek from God what is against his decree? They pray according to his will, not that hidden and unchangeable will but the will that he inspires in them, that he may hearken to them in another way, as he wisely decides." Rightly said. For he so tempers the outcome of events according to his incomprehensible plan that the prayers of the saints, which are a mixture of faith and error, are not nullified. But this ought no more to be held as a valid example for imitation than as excusing the saints themselves; that they exceeded due measure,

I do not deny. Therefore, where no certain promise shows itself, we must ask of God conditionally. Here that statement of David is appropriate: "Awake ... unto the judgement which you have commanded" [Ps 7:6]. For he shows that he was instructed by a special oracle to seek a temporal benefit.

Our prayers can obtain an answer only through God's forgiveness
This also is worth noting: what I have set forth on the four rules of right praying is not so rigorously required that God will reject those prayers in which he finds neither perfect faith nor repentance, together with a warmth of zeal and petitions rightly conceived.

I have said that, although prayer is an intimate conversation of the pious with God, yet reverence and moderation must be kept, lest we give loose rein to miscellaneous requests, and lest we crave more than God allows; further, that we should lift up our minds to a pure and chaste veneration of him, lest God's majesty become worthless for us.

No-one has ever carried this out with the uprightness that was due; for, not to mention the rank and file, how many complaints of David savour of intemperance! Not that he would either deliberately argue with God or clamour against his judgements, but that, fainting with weakness, he finds no other solace better than to cast his own sorrows into the bosom of God. But God tolerates even our stammering and pardons our ignorance whenever something inadvertently escapes us; as indeed without this mercy there would be no freedom to pray. But although David intended to submit completely to God's will, and prayed with no less patience than zeal to obtain his request, yet there come forth—sometimes, rather, boil up—turbulent emotions, quite out of harmony with the first rule that we laid down.

We can especially see from the ending of the thirty-ninth Psalm with what violent sorrow this holy man is carried away, so that he cannot control himself. "Let me alone", he says, "before I depart, and be no more". One might say that this desperate man seeks nothing except to rot in his evils, with God's hand withdrawn. Not that he deliberately rushes into that intemperance, or, as the wicked are inclined to do, wishes to be far from God, but he only complains that God's wrath is unbearable. In those trials also there are often uttered petitions not sufficiently consistent with the rule of God's Word, and in which the saints do not sufficiently weigh what is lawful and expedient. All prayers marred by these defects deserve to be repudiated; nevertheless, provided the saints bemoan their sins, chastise themselves, and immediately return to themselves, God pardons them.

They likewise sin with regard to the second rule; for they must repeatedly wrestle with their own coldness, and their need and misery do not sharply enough urge them to pray earnestly. Now it often happens that their minds slip away and well-nigh vanish; accordingly, in this respect there is also need for pardon, lest our languid or mutilated, or interrupted and vague, prayers suffer a refusal. God has planted in men's minds by nature the principle that their prayers are lawful only when their minds are uplifted. Hence the rite of lifting up the hands, to which we have previously referred—one common to all ages and peoples, and still in force. But how rarely is there one who, in raising up his hands, is not aware of his own apathy, since his heart stays on the ground?

With regard to seeking forgiveness of sins, although no believers neglect this topic, yet those truly versed in prayers know that they do not offer the tenth part of that sacrifice of which David speaks: "The sacrifice acceptable to God is a broken spirit; a contrite and humbled heart, O God, you will not despise" [Ps 51:17]. Accordingly, men should always seek a twofold pardon because they are aware of many offences, the feeling of which still does not so touch them that they are as much displeased with themselves as they ought to be, but also because, in so far as it has been granted them to benefit by repentance and fear of God, stricken down with a just sorrow on account of their offences, they pray that the wrath of the judge be averted.

Most of all it is weakness or imperfection of faith that contaminates believers' prayers, unless God's mercy help them; but no wonder God pardons this defect, since he often tests his own with sharp trials, as if he deliberately willed to snuff out their faith. Hardest of all is this trial, where believers are compelled to cry out, "How long will you be angry with the prayer of your servant?" [Ps 80:4], as if prayers themselves annoyed God. So when Jeremiah says, "God has shut out my prayer" [Lam 3:8], there is no doubt that he was stricken with violent agitation. Innumerable examples of this kind occur in Scripture, from which it is clear the faith of the saints was often so mixed and troubled with doubts that in believing and hoping they yet betrayed some want of faith. But because they do not reach the goal desired, they ought the more to endeavour to correct their faults, and each day come nearer to the perfect rule of prayer. Meanwhile they should also feel the depths of evil in which some people have been plunged, who bring new diseases upon themselves in their very remedies. After all, there is no prayer which in justice God would not loathe, if he did not overlook the spots with which all are sprinkled. I do not recount these matters in order that believers may confidently pardon themselves for anything, but that by severely chastising themselves they may strive to overcome these obstacles. Although Satan tries to block all paths to prevent them from praying, they should nonetheless break through, surely persuaded that, although not freed of all hindrances, their efforts still please God and their petitions are approved, provided they endeavour and strive toward a goal not immediately attainable.

The intercession of Christ

Prayer in the name of Jesus

Since no man is worthy to present himself to God and come into his sight, the Heavenly Father himself, to free us at once from shame and fear, which might well have thrown our hearts into despair, has given us his Son, Jesus Christ our Lord, to be our advocate and mediator with him. By Christ's guidance we may confidently come to him. With such an intercessor we trust that nothing we ask in his name will be denied us, as nothing can be denied to him by the Father. To this must be referred all that we previously taught about faith. For just as the promise commends Christ the Mediator to us, so, unless the hope of obtaining our requests depends upon him, it cuts itself off from the benefit of prayer.

For as soon as God's dread majesty comes to mind, we cannot but tremble and be driven far away by the recognition of our own unworthiness, until Christ comes forward as intermediary, to change the throne of dreadful glory into the throne of grace. The apostle also teaches how we should dare with all confidence to appear, to receive mercy, and to find grace in timely help. And as a rule has been established to call upon God, and a promise given that those who call upon him shall be heard, so too we are particularly bidden to call upon him in Christ's name; and we have the promise made that we shall obtain what we have asked in his name. "Until now", he says, "you have asked nothing in my name; ask and you will receive" [John 16:24]. "In that day you will ask in my name" [John 16:26], and "whatever you ask ... I will do it that the Father may be glorified in the Son" [John 14:13].

Hence it is incontrovertibly clear that those who call upon God in another name than that of Christ obstinately flout his commands and count his will as worthless—indeed, have no promise of obtaining anything. Indeed, as Paul says, "all God's promises find their yes and amen in him" [2 Cor 1:20]. That is, they are confirmed and fulfilled.

The risen Christ as our intercessor

And we ought carefully to note the circumstance of the time when Christ enjoins his disciples to take refuge in his intercession, after he shall have ascended into heaven. "In that hour", he says, "you will ask in my name" [John 16:26].

It is certain that, from the beginning, those who prayed were not heard save by the Mediator's grace. For this reason, God had taught in the law that the priest alone entering the sanctuary should bear the names of the tribes of Israel upon his shoulders and the same number of precious stones on his breastplate, but the people should stand afar off in the court, and there join their petitions with the priest. Nay, the sacrifice even had value in ratifying and strengthening the prayers. Therefore, that foreshadowing ceremony of the law taught us that we are all barred from God's presence, and consequently need a Mediator, who should appear in our name and bear us upon his shoulders and hold us bound upon his breast so that we are heard in his person; further, that our prayers are cleansed by sprinkled blood—prayers that, as has been stated, are otherwise never free of uncleanness. And we see that the saints, when they desired to obtain something, based their hope on sacrifices, for they knew them to be the sanctions of all petitions. "May he remember your offering", says David, "and make your burnt sacrifice fat" [Ps 20:3]. Hence we infer that God was from the beginning appeased by Christ's intercession, so that he received the petitions of the godly.

Why, then, does Christ assign a new hour wherein his disciples shall begin to pray in his name unless it is that this grace, as it is more resplendent today, so deserves more approval among us? And he had said a little before in the same sense: "Until now you have asked nothing in my name; ask" [John 16:24]. Not that they understand absolutely nothing about the office of Mediator, since all the Jews were steeped in these rudiments, but because they did not yet clearly understand that Christ by his very ascension into heaven would be a surer advocate of the church than he had been before. Therefore, to console their grief at his absence with some uncommon benefit, he takes upon himself the office of advocate, and teaches that they had beforehand lacked the peculiar blessing that will be given them to enjoy when, relying upon his protection, they more freely call upon God. Thus the apostle says that the new way is consecrated by his blood [Heb 10:20]. The less excusable is our perversity unless we embrace with both arms, as the saying is, this truly inestimable benefit, which is destined for us alone.

Christ is the only Mediator, even for the mutual intercession of believers
Now, since he is the only way, and the one access, by which it is granted us to come to God, to those who turn aside from this way and forsake this access, no way and no access to God remain; nothing is left in his throne but wrath, judgement, and terror. Moreover, since the Father has sealed him as our

head and leader, those who in any way turn aside or incline away from him are trying their level best to destroy and disfigure the mark imprinted by God. Thus Christ is constituted the only Mediator, by whose intercession the Father is for us rendered gracious and easily entreated.

Meanwhile, notwithstanding, the saints still retain their intercessions, whereby they commend one another's salvation to God. The apostle mentions these [1 Tim 2:1], but all depend solely upon Christ's intercession, so far are they from detracting from his in any way. For as they gush forth from the emotion of love, in which we willingly and freely embrace one another as members of one body, so also are they related to the unity of the head. When, therefore, those intercessions are also made in Christ's name, what else do they attest but that no-one can be helped by any prayers at all save when Christ intercedes? Christ does not by his intercession hinder us from pleading for one another by prayers in the church. So, then, let it remain an established principle that we should direct all intercessions of the whole church to that sole intercession. Indeed, especially for this reason should we beware of ungratefulness, because God, pardoning our unworthiness, not only allows individuals to pray for themselves but also permits men to plead for one another. For when God has appointed advocates of his church who deserve to be duly rejected if each one prays exclusively for himself, what sheer presumption is it to abuse this generosity so as to dim Christ's honour?

Kinds of prayer: private and public

Private prayer

But even though prayer is properly confined to entreaties and supplications, there is such a close connection between petition and thanksgiving that they may conveniently be included under one name. For those kinds which Paul lists fall under the first part of this division. In asking and beseeching, we pour out our desires before God, seeking both those things which make for the extension of his glory and the setting forth of his name, and those benefits which conduce to our own advantage. In giving thanks, we celebrate with due praise his benefits toward us, and credit to his generosity every good that comes to us.

David, therefore, has combined these two functions: "Call upon me in the day of need; I will deliver you, and you shall glorify me" [Ps 50:15]. Scripture with good reason enjoins us to use both constantly. For as we have stated elsewhere, the weight of our poverty and the facts of experience proclaim that the tribulations which drive and press us from all sides are so many and so great that there is reason enough for us all continually to groan and sigh to God, and to beseech him as beggars. For even if they be free of troubles, the guilt of their transgressions and the innumerable assaults of temptations ought still to incite even the holiest to seek a remedy. But in the sacrifice of praise and thanksgiving there can be no interruption without sin, since God does not cease to heap benefits upon benefits in order to impel us, though slow and lazy, to gratefulness. In short, we are well-nigh overwhelmed by so great and so plenteous an outpouring of benefactions, by so many and mighty miracles discerned wherever one looks, that we never lack reason and occasion for praise and thanksgiving.

And to explain these things somewhat more clearly, since, as has already been sufficiently proved, all our hope and wealth so reside in God that neither we nor our possessions prosper unless we can have his blessing, we ought constantly to commit ourselves and all that we have to him. Then whatever we determine, speak, do, let us determine, speak, and do under his hand and will—in a word, under the hope of his help. For all are declared accursed by God who, placing confidence in themselves or someone else, conceive and carry out their plans; who undertake or try to begin anything apart from his will, and without calling upon him. And since, as we have said several times, he is honoured in the manner due him when he is acknowledged the author of all blessings, it follows that we ought so to receive all those things from his hand as to accompany them with continual thanksgiving; and that there is no just reason for us to make use of his benefits, which flow and come to us from his generosity, with no other end, if we do not continually utter his praise and render him thanks. For Paul, when he testifies that they "are sanctified by the word ... and prayer" [1 Tim 4:5], at the same time hints that without the word and prayer they are not at all holy and pure for us. ('Word' he evidently understands, by association, as 'faith'.) Accordingly, David, when he has perceived the Lord's generosity, beautifully declares a "new song" has been put into his mouth [Ps 40:3]. By this he naturally hints that if we fail to offer him praise for his blessing, our silence is spiteful, since as often as he blesses us he provides us with occasion to bless him. So Isaiah also, proclaiming God's singular grace, urges believers to a new and uncommon song [Isa 42:10]. In this sense, David elsewhere speaks: "O Lord, open my lips, and my mouth shall show forth your praise" [Ps 51:15]. In like manner, Hezekiah and Jonah testify that this will be the outcome of their deliverance: that they may sing the praises of God's goodness in the Temple [Isa 38:20; Jonah 2:9]. David prescribes the same rule to all the godly in common. "What shall I render to the

Lord", he says, "for all his bounty to me? I will lift up the cup of salvation and call on the name of the Lord" [Ps 116:12-13]. And the church follows this rule in another psalm: "Make us safe, O our God … that we may confess your … name, and glory in your praise" [Ps 106:47]. Again: "He has had regard for the prayer of the solitary, and has not despised their prayers. This will be written for a later generation, and the people created shall praise the Lord … to proclaim his name in Zion, and his praise in Jerusalem" [Ps 102:17-18, 21]. Indeed, whenever believers entreat God to do something for his name's sake, as they profess themselves unworthy to obtain anything in their own name, so they obligate themselves to give thanks; and they promise that they will rightly use God's benefit, to be the heralds of it. So Hosea, speaking of the coming redemption of the Church: "Take away", he says, "iniquity, O God, and accept that which is good" [Hos 14:2].

Not only do God's benefits claim for themselves the extolling by the tongue, but also they naturally win love for themselves. "I loved the Lord", says David, "because he heard the voice of my petition" [Ps 116:1]. Also, elsewhere recounting what help he had experienced: "I shall love you, O God, my strength" [Ps 18:1]. But praises that do not flow from this sweetness of love will never please God. Even more, we must understand Paul's statement that all entreaties not joined with thanksgiving are wicked and vicious. For he speaks thus: "In all prayer and supplication with thanksgiving let your petitions be made known to God" [Phil 4:6]. For since many by peevishness, boredom, impatience, bitter grief, and fear are impelled to mumble when praying, he bids believers so to temper their emotions that while still waiting to obtain what they desire, they nonetheless cheerfully bless God. But if this connection ought to be in full force in things almost contrary, by a still holier bond God obligates us to sing his praises whenever he causes us to obtain our wishes.

Now even as we have taught that by Christ's intercession are consecrated our prayers, which would otherwise have been unclean, so the apostle, enjoining us to offer a sacrifice of praise through Christ, warns us that our mouths are not clean enough to sing the praises of God's name until Christ's priesthood intercedes for us. We infer from this that in the papacy men have been strangely bewitched, since the majority of them wonder why Christ is called "the Advocate".

The reason why Paul enjoins us both to pray and to give thanks without ceasing is, of course, that he wishes all men to lift up their desires to God, with all possible constancy, at all times, in all places, and in all affairs and transactions, to expect all things from him, and give him praise for all things, since he offers us unfailing reasons to praise and pray.

Necessity and danger of public prayer
This constancy in prayer, even though it has especially to do with one's own private prayers, still is also concerned somewhat with the public prayers of the church. Yet these can neither be constant nor ought they even to take place otherwise than according to the polity agreed upon by common consent among all. This I grant you. For this reason, certain hours, indifferent to God but necessary for men's convenience, are agreed upon and appointed to provide for the accommodation of all, and for everything to be done "decently and in order" in the church, according to Paul's statement. But this does not preclude each church from being both repeatedly stirred up to more frequent use of prayer and fired by a sharper zeal if it is alerted by some major need. There will be,

moreover, toward the end, a place to speak of perseverance, which has close affinity with constancy.

Now these matters have nothing to do with the vain repetition that Christ willed to be forbidden to us. For Christ does not forbid us to persist in prayers, long, often, or with much feeling, but requires that we should not be confident in our ability to wrest something from God by beating upon his ears with a garrulous flow of talk, as if he could be persuaded as men are. For we know that hypocrites, because they do not reflect that they have to do with God, make the same pompous show in prayers as they would in a triumph. For that Pharisee who thanked God that he was not like other men [Luke 18:11] doubtless praised himself in men's eyes, as if he would from praying latch on to renown for holiness. Hence that vain repetition which for a similar reason is in vogue today in the papacy. While some pass the time in saying over and over the same little prayers, others vaunt themselves before the crowd with a great mass of words. Since this talkativeness childishly mocks God, it is no wonder that it is forbidden by the church in order that nothing shall resound there except what is earnest and comes forth from the depths of the heart.

Near and similar to this corrupt element is another, which Christ condemns at the same time: hypocrites, for the sake of show, pant after many witnesses, and would rather frequent the market place to pray than have their prayers miss the world's applause. But inasmuch as this goal of prayer has already been stated—namely, that hearts may be aroused and borne to God, whether to praise him or to beseech his help—from this we may understand that the essentials of prayer are set in the mind and heart, or rather that prayer itself is properly an emotion of the heart within, which is poured out and laid open before God, the searcher of hearts. Accordingly, as has already been said, the Heavenly Teacher, when he willed to lay down the best rule for prayer, bade us enter into our bedroom and there, with door closed, pray to our Father in secret, that our Father, who is in secret, may hear us [Matt 6:6]. For, when he has drawn us away from the example of hypocrites, who grasped after the favour of men by vain and ostentatious prayers, he at the same time adds something better: that is, to enter into our bedroom and there, with door closed, pray. By these words, as I understand them, he taught us to seek a retreat that would help us to descend into our heart with our whole thought and enter deeply within. He promises that God, whose temples our bodies ought to be, will be near to us in the affections of our hearts.

For he did not mean to deny that it is fitting to pray in other places, but he shows that prayer is something secret, which is both principally lodged in the heart and requires a tranquillity far from all our teeming cares. The Lord himself also, therefore, with good reason, when he determined to devote himself more intensely to prayers, habitually withdrew to a quiet spot far away from the tumult of men; but he did so to impress us with his example that we must not neglect these helps, whereby our mind, too unsteady by itself, more inclines to earnest application to prayer. In the meantime, as he did not abstain from praying even in the midst of a crowd if the occasion so presented itself, so we should lift up clean hands in all places, where there is need. Finally, we must consider that whoever refused to pray in the holy assembly of the godly knows not what it is to pray individually, or in a secret spot, or at home. Again, he who neglects to pray alone and in private, however unremittingly he may frequent public assemblies, there contrives only windy prayers, for he defers more to the opinion of men than to the secret judgement of God.

Moreover, that the common prayers of the church may not be held in contempt, God of old adorned them with shining titles, especially when he called the temple the "house of prayer". For he taught by this term that the chief part of his worship lies in the office of prayer, and that the temple was set up like a banner for believers so that they might, with one consent, participate in it. A distinctive promise was also added: "Praise waits for you, O God, in Zion, and to you shall the vow be performed" [Ps 65:1]. By these words the prophet intimates that the prayers of the church are never ineffectual, for God always furnishes his people occasion for singing with joy. But even though the shadows of the law have ceased, still there is no doubt that the same promise pertains to us, since God was pleased by this ceremony to foster the unity of the faith among us. For not only has Christ sanctioned this promise by his own mouth, but Paul holds it to be universally in force.

Not church buildings but we ourselves are temples of God
Now as God by his word ordains common prayers for believers, so also ought there to be public temples wherein these may be performed, in which those who spurn fellowship with God's people in prayer have no occasion to give the false excuse that they enter their bedroom to obey the Lord's command. For he, who promises that he will do whatever two or three gathered together in his name may ask, testifies that he does not despise prayers publicly made, provided ostentation and chasing after paltry human glory are banished, and there is present sincere and true affection that dwells in the secret place of the heart.

If this is the lawful use of church buildings, as it certainly is, we in turn must guard against either taking them to be God's proper dwelling places, whence he may more nearly incline his ear to us—as they began to be regarded some centuries ago—or feigning for them some secret holiness or other, which would render prayer more sacred before God. For since we ourselves are God's true temples, if we would call upon God in his holy temple, we must pray within ourselves. Now let us leave this stupidity to Jews or pagans, for we have the commandment to call upon the Lord, without distinction of place, "in spirit and in truth" [John 4:23]. At God's command the Temple had indeed been dedicated of old for offering prayers and sacrificial victims, but at that time the truth lay hidden, figuratively represented under such shadows; now, having been expressed to us in living reality, it does not allow us to cleave to any material temple. And not even to the Jews was the Temple committed on the condition that they might shut up God's presence within its walls but in order that they might be trained to contemplate the likeness of the true temple. Therefore Isaiah and Stephen gravely rebuked those who thought God in any way dwells in temples made with hands [Isa 66:1; Acts 7:48-49].

The use of singing, and of the spoken language
On speaking and singing in prayer
From this, moreover, it is fully evident that unless voice and song, if interposed in prayer, spring from deep feeling of heart, neither has any value or profit in the least with God. But they arouse his wrath against us if they come only from the tip of the lips and from the throat, seeing that this is to abuse his most holy name and to hold his majesty in derision. This is what we gather from Isaiah's words, which, although

they extend farther, also are concerned with reproving this fault. "The people", he says, "draw near to me with their mouth, and honour me with their lips, but their hearts are far from me, and they have feared me by the command and teaching of men" [Isa 29:13]. "Therefore, behold, I will ... do a great and marvellous miracle among this people; for the wisdom of their wise men shall perish, and the prudence of their elders shall vanish" [Isa 29:14].

Yet we do not here condemn speaking and singing but rather strongly commend them, provided they are associated with the heart's affection. For thus do they exercise the mind in thinking of God and keep it attentive—unstable and variable as it is, and readily relaxed and diverted in different directions, unless it be supported by various helps. Moreover, since the glory of God ought, in a measure, to shine in the several parts of our bodies, it is especially fitting that the tongue has been assigned and destined for this task, both through singing and through speaking. For it was peculiarly created to tell and proclaim the praise of God. But the chief use of the tongue is in public prayers, which are offered in the assembly of believers, by which it comes about that with one common voice, and as it were, with the same mouth, we all glorify God together, worshipping him with one spirit and the same faith. And we do this openly, that all men mutually, each one from his brother, may receive the confession of faith and be invited and prompted by his example.

Church singing
It is evident that the practice of singing in church, to speak also of this in passing, is not only a very ancient one but also was in use among the apostles. This we may infer from Paul's words: "I will sing with the spirit and I will sing with

the mind" [1 Cor 14:15]. Likewise, Paul speaks to the Colossians: "Teaching and admonishing one another … in hymns, psalms, and spiritual songs, singing with thankfulness in your hearts to the Lord" [Col 3:16]. For in the first passage he teaches that we should sing with voice and heart; in the second he commends spiritual songs, by which the godly may mutually edify one another.

Yet Augustine testifies that this practice was not universal when he states that the church of Milan first began to sing only under Ambrose; the occasion being that when Justina, the mother of Valentinian, was raging against the orthodox faith, the people were more constant in vigils than usual. Then the remaining Western churches followed Milan. For a little before he had said that this custom had come from the Eastern churches. He also indicates in the second book of his *Retractations* that the practice was taken up in Africa in his day. "A certain Hilary", he says, "an ex-tribune, attacked with malicious reproof, wherever he could, the custom, then just begun at Carthage, of singing hymns from the book of Psalms at the altar, either before the offering or when what had been offered was being distributed to the people. At the bidding of my brethren, I answered him."

And surely, if the singing be tempered to that gravity which is fitting in the sight of God and the angels, it both lends dignity and grace to sacred actions and has the greatest value in kindling our hearts to a true zeal and eagerness to pray. Yet we should be very careful that our ears be not more attentive to the melody than our minds to the spiritual meaning of the words. Augustine also admits in another place that he was so disturbed by this danger that he sometimes wished to see established the custom observed by Athanasius, who ordered the reader to use so little inflection of the voice that he would sound more like a speaker than a singer. But when he recalled how much benefit singing had brought him, he inclined to the other side. Therefore, when this moderation is maintained, it is without any doubt a most holy and salutary practice. On the other hand, such songs as have been composed only for sweetness and delight of the ear are unbecoming to the majesty of the church and cannot but displease God in the highest degree.

Prayer should be in the language of the people
From this also it plainly appears that public prayers must not be in Greek among the Latins, nor in Latin among the French or English, as has previously been the custom, but in the language of the people, which can be generally understood by the whole assembly. For this ought to be done for the edification of the whole church, which receives no benefit whatever from a sound not understood. Those who have no regard for either love or kindliness ought at least to have been moved a little by the authority of Paul, whose words are perfectly clear. "If you bless with the spirit", he says, "how can he who occupies the place of the unlearned respond to your blessing with 'Amen', since he is ignorant of what you are saying? For you indeed give thanks, but the other is not edified" [1 Cor 14:16-17]. Who can marvel enough, then, at the unbridled licence of the papists, who, after the apostle thus openly decries it, are not afraid to make their wordy prayers resound in a foreign language, of which they themselves often understand not one syllable, and do not wish others to understand either?

But for us Paul prescribes otherwise what is to be done. "What am I to do?" he says. "I will pray with the spirit, I will pray with the mind also; I will sing with the spirit and I will sing with the mind also" [1 Cor 14:15]. By the word "spirit" he means the singular gift of tongues, which some, though they were endowed with it, abused, since they cut it off from the mind, that is, the understanding. However, we must unquestionably feel that, either in public prayer or in private, the tongue without the mind must be highly displeasing to God. Besides, the mind ought to be kindled with an ardour of thought so as far to surpass all that the tongue can express by speaking.

Lastly, we should hold that the tongue is not even necessary for private prayer, except in so far as either the inner feeling has insufficient power to arouse itself or as it is so vehemently aroused that it carries with it the action of the tongue. For even though the best prayers are sometimes unspoken, it often happens in practice that, when feelings of mind are aroused, unostentatiously the tongue breaks forth into speech, and the other members into gesture. From this obviously arose that uncertain murmur of Hannah's [1 Sam 1:13], something similar to which all the saints continually experience when they burst forth into broken and fragmentary speech.

As for the bodily gestures customarily observed in praying, such as kneeling and uncovering the head, they are exercises whereby we try to rise to a greater reverence for God.

The Lord's Prayer: exposition of the first three petitions
The Lord's Prayer as necessary help for us

Now we must learn not only a more certain way of praying but also the form itself: namely, that which the Heavenly Father has taught us through his beloved Son [Matt 6:9ff.; Luke 11:2ff.], in which we may acknowledge his boundless goodness and mercy. For he warns us and urges us to seek him in our every need, as children take refuge in the protection of the parents whenever they are troubled with any anxiety. Besides this, since he saw that we did not even sufficiently perceive how great our poverty was, what it was fair to request, and what was profitable for us, he also provided for this ignorance of ours; and what had been lacking to our capacity he himself supplied and made sufficient from his own. For he prescribed a form for us in which he set forth as in a table all that he allows us to seek of him, all that is of benefit to us, all that we need ask. From this kindness of his we receive great fruit of consolation: that we know we are requesting nothing absurd, nothing strange or unseemly— in short, nothing unacceptable to him—since we are asking almost in his own words. Plato, on seeing men's want of skill in making requests to God, which, if granted, would often have been disadvantageous to them, declares this, taken from an ancient poet, to be the best prayer: "King Jupiter, bestow the best things upon us whether we wish for them or not, but command that evil things be far from us even when we request them". And, indeed, the heathen man is wise in that he judges how dangerous it is to seek from the Lord what our greed dictates; at the same time he discloses our unhappiness, in that we cannot even open our mouths before God without danger unless the Spirit instructs us in the right pattern for prayer. This privilege deserves to be more highly esteemed among us, since the only begotten Son of God supplies words to our lips that free our minds from all wavering.

Division and main content
This form or rule of prayer consists of six petitions. The reason why I do not agree with those who distinguish seven headings is that by inserting "but" the Evangelist seems to

have meant to join those two phrases together. It is as if he had said: "Do not allow us to be oppressed by temptation but rather bring help for our weakness, and deliver us from falling". Ancient writers of the church also agree with us, so that what has been added in seventh place in Matthew exegetically ought to be referred to the sixth petition.

But even though the whole prayer is such that throughout it God's glory is to be given chief place, still the first three petitions have been particularly assigned to God's glory, and this alone we ought to look to in them, without consideration of what is called our own advantage. The three others are concerned with the care of ourselves, and are especially assigned to those things which we should ask for our own benefit. So, when we ask that God's name be hallowed, because God wills to test us whether we love and worship him freely or for hope of reward, we must then have no consideration for our own benefit but must set before ourselves his glory, to gaze with eyes intent upon this one thing. And in the remaining petitions of this sort, it is fitting to be affected in precisely the same way.

And, indeed, this yields a great benefit to us, because when his name is hallowed as we ask, our own hallowing in turn also comes about. But our eyes ought, as it were, to be closed and in a sense blinded to this sort of advantage, so that they have no regard for it at all, and so that, if all hope of our own private good were cut off, still we should not cease to desire and entreat this hallowing and the other things that pertain to God's glory. In the examples of Moses and Paul, we see that it was not grievous for them to turn their minds and eyes away from themselves and to long for their own destruction with fierce and burning zeal in order that, despite their own loss, they might advance God's glory and Kingdom [Ex 32:32; Rom 9:3]. On the other hand, when we ask to be given our daily bread, even though we desire what is to our benefit, here also we ought especially to seek God's glory so as not to ask it unless it contribute to his glory. Now let us turn to the interpretation of the prayer.

"Our Father"

First, at the very threshold we meet what I previously mentioned: we ought to offer all prayer to God only in Christ's name, as it cannot be agreeable to him in any other name. For in calling God "Father", we put forward the name "Christ". With what confidence would anyone address God as "Father"? Who would break forth into such rashness as to claim for himself the honour of a son of God unless we had been adopted as children of grace in Christ? He, while he is the true Son, has of himself been given us as a brother that what he has of his own by nature may become ours by benefit of adoption if we embrace this great blessing with sure faith. Accordingly, John says that power has been given to those who believe in the name of the only-begotten Son of God, that they too may become children of God [John 1:12].

Therefore God both calls himself our Father and would have us so address him. By the great sweetness of this name he frees us from all distrust, since no greater feeling of love can be found elsewhere than in the Father. Therefore he could not attest his own boundless love toward us with any surer proof than the fact that we are called "children of God" [1 John 3:1]. But just as he surpasses all men in goodness and mercy, so is his love greater and more excellent than all our parents' love. Hence, though all earthly fathers should divest themselves of all feeling of fatherhood and forsake their children, he will never fail us, since he cannot deny himself. For we have his promise: "If you, although you are evil, know how to give good gifts to your children, how much more will your Father, who is in heaven?" [Matt 7:11].

Similarly, in the prophet: "Can a woman forget her ... children? ... Even if she forgets, yet I shall not forget you" [Isa 49:15]. But a son cannot give himself over to the safe-keeping of a stranger and an alien without at the same time complaining either of his father's cruelty or want. Thus, if we are his sons, we cannot seek help anywhere else than from him without reproaching him for poverty, or want of means, or cruelty and excessive rigour.

"Our Father": a form of address that should encourage us

And let us not pretend that we are justly rendered timid by the consciousness of sins, since sins daily make our Father, although kind and gentle, displeased with us. For if among men, a son can have no better advocate to plead his cause before his father, can have no better intermediary to conciliate and recover his lost favour, than if he himself, contrite and humble, acknowledging his guilt, implores his father's mercy—for then his father's heart cannot pretend to be moved by such entreaties—what will he do who is the Father of mercies and God of all comfort? Will he not rather heed the tears and groans of his children entreating for themselves, since he particularly invites and exhorts us to this, than any pleas of others, to whose help they in terror have recourse, not without some signs of despair, since they are distrustful of their Father's compassion and kindness? He depicts and represents for us in a parable this abundance of fatherly compassion: a son had estranged himself from his father, had dissolutely wasted his substance, had grievously offended against him in every way; but the father embraces him with open arms, and does not wait for him to ask for pardon but anticipates him, recognizes him returning afar off, willingly runs to meet him, comforts him, receives him into favour. For in setting forth this example of great compassion to be seen in man, he willed to teach us how much more abundantly we ought to expect it of him. For he is not only a father but by far the best and kindest of all fathers, provided we still cast ourselves upon his mercy, although we are ungrateful, rebellious, and wilful children. And to strengthen our assurance that he is this sort of father to us if we are Christians, he willed that we call him not only "Father" but explicitly "our Father". It is as if we addressed him: "O Father, who abounds with great devotion toward your children, and with great readiness to forgive, we your children call upon you and make our prayer, assured and clearly persuaded that you bear toward us only the affection of a father, although we are unworthy of such a father".

But because the narrowness of our hearts cannot comprehend God's boundless favour, not only is Christ the pledge and guarantee of our adoption, but he gives the Spirit as witness to us of the same adoption, through whom with free and full voice we may cry, "Abba, Father" [Rom 8:15]. Therefore, whenever any hesitation shall hinder us, let us remember to ask him to correct our fearfulness, and to set before us that Spirit that he may guide us to pray boldly.

"Our Father": a form of address that sets us in the fellowship with the brethren
However, we are not so instructed that each one of us should individually call him his Father, but rather that all of us in common should call him our Father. From this fact we are warned how great a feeling of brotherly love ought to be

among us, since by the same right of mercy and free liberality we are equally children of such a father. For if one father is common to us all, and every good thing that can fall to our lot comes from him, there ought not to be anything separate among us that we are not prepared gladly and wholeheartedly to share with one another, as far as occasion requires.

Now if we so desire, as is fitting, to extend our hand to one another and to help one another, there is nothing in which we can benefit our brethren more than in commending them to the providential care of the best of fathers; for if he is kind and favourable, nothing at all else can be desired. Indeed, we owe even this very thing to our Father. Just as one who truly and deeply loves any father of a family at the same time embraces his whole household with love and good will, so it becomes us in like measure to show to his people, to his family, and lastly, to his inheritance, the same zeal and affection that we have toward this Heavenly Father. For he so honoured these as to call them the fullness of his only-begotten Son. Let the Christian man, then, conform his prayers to this rule in order that they may be in common and embrace all who are his brothers in Christ, not only those whom he at present sees and recognizes as such but all men who dwell on earth. For what God has determined concerning them is beyond our knowing except that it is no less godly than humane to wish and hope the best for them. Yet we ought to be drawn with a special affection to those, above others, of the household of faith, whom the apostle has particularly commended to us in everything. To sum up, all prayers ought to be such as to look to that community which our Lord has established in his Kingdom and his household.

Comparison of prayer and almsgiving

Nevertheless, this does not prevent us from praying especially for ourselves and for certain others, provided, however, our minds do not withdraw their attention from this community or turn aside from it but refer all things to it. For although prayers are individually framed, since they are directed to this end, they do not cease to be common. All this can easily be understood by a comparison. There is a general command of God's to relieve the need of all the poor, and yet those obey it who to this end give aid to those whom they know or see to be suffering, even though they overlook many who are pressed by no lighter need because either they cannot know all or cannot provide for all. In this way, people who frame particular prayers of this sort because they view and ponder the common society of the church, do not resist the will of God when in their prayers, with God's people at heart, in particular terms, they commend to God themselves or others whose needs he has been pleased to make intimately known to them.

However, not all aspects of prayer and almsgiving are indeed alike. For liberality of giving can be practised only toward those whose poverty is visible to us. But we are free to help by prayer even utterly foreign and unknown persons, however great the distance that separates them from us. This, too, is done through that general form of prayer wherein all children of God are included, among whom they also are. To this may be referred the fact that Paul urges the believers of his time to lift pure hands in every place without quarrelling. In warning them that strife shuts the gate to prayers, his intention is that they offer their petitions in common with one accord.

"Our Father ... in heaven"

That he is in heaven is added. From this we are not immediately to reason that he is bound, shut up, and surrounded, by the circumference of heaven, as by a barred enclosure. For Solomon confesses that the heaven of heavens cannot contain him. And he himself says through the prophet that heaven is his seat, and the earth, his footstool. By this he obviously means that he is not confined to any particular region but is diffused through all things. But our minds, so crass are they, could not have conceived his unspeakable glory otherwise. Consequently, it has been signified to us by "heaven", for we can behold nothing more sublime or majestic than this. While, therefore, wherever our senses comprehend anything they commonly attach it to that place, God is set beyond all place, so that when we would seek him we must rise above all perception of body and soul. Secondly, by this expression he is lifted above all chance of either corruption or change. Finally, it signifies that he embraces and holds together the entire universe and controls it by his might. Therefore it is as if he had been said to be of infinite greatness or loftiness, of incomprehensible essence, of boundless might, and of everlasting immortality. But while we hear this, our thought must be raised higher when God is spoken of, lest we dream up anything earthly or physical about him, lest we measure him by our small measure, or conform his will to our emotions. At the same time our confidence in him must be aroused, since we understand that heaven and earth are ruled by his providence and power.

To sum up: under the name "Father" is set before us that God who appeared to us in his own image that we should call upon him with assured faith. And not only does the intimate name "Father" engender trust but it is effective also to keep our minds from being drawn away to doubtful and false gods, permitting them to rise up from the only-begotten Son to the sole Father of angels and of the church. Secondly, because his throne is established in heaven, from his governing of the universe we are forcibly reminded that we do not come to him in vain, for he willingly meets us with present help. "Those who draw near to God", says the apostle, "must first believe that God exists, then that he rewards all who seek him" [Heb 11:6]. Here Christ declares both of these things to his Father: that our faith rests in himself, then that we should surely be persuaded that our salvation is not overlooked by him. For he deigns to extend his providence even to us. By this elementary instruction Paul prepares us to pray properly. For before enjoining us to make our petitions known to God, he thus prefaces the injunction: "Have no anxiety about anything"; "the Lord is at hand" [Phil 4:5, 6]. From this it is clear that those who do not feel assured that "God's eye is upon the righteous" [Ps 34:15] in doubt and perplexity turn ever their prayers within their minds.

The first petition

The first petition is that God's name be hallowed; the need for it is associated with our great shame. For what is more unworthy than for God's glory to be obscured partly by our ungratefulness, partly by our ill will, and so far as lies in our power, destroyed by our presumption and insane impudence? Though all ungodly men should break out with their sacrilegious licence, the holiness of God's name still shines. The prophet justifiably proclaims: "As your name, O God, so your praise to all the ends of the earth" [Ps 48:10]. For wherever God becomes known, his powers cannot fail to be manifested; might, goodness, wisdom, righteousness, mercy, truth—these should captivate us with wonderment for him, and impel us to celebrate his praise. Because, therefore, God's holiness is so unworthily snatched from him on earth, if it is not in our power to assert it, at least we are bidden to be concerned for it in our prayers.

To summarize: we should wish God to have the honour he deserves; men should never speak or think of him without the highest reverence. To this is opposed the profanity that has always been too common and even today is abroad in the world. Hence the need of this petition, which ought to have been superfluous if even a little godliness existed among us. But if holiness is associated with God's name where separated from all other names it breathes pure glory, here we are bidden to request not only that God vindicate his sacred name of all contempt and dishonour but also that he subdue the whole race of mankind to reverence for it.

Now since God reveals himself to us partly in teaching, partly in works, we can hallow him only if we render to him what is his in both respects, and so embrace all that proceeds from him. And his sternness no less than his leniency should lead us to praise him, seeing that he has engraved marks of his glory upon a manifold diversity of works, and this rightly calls forth praises from every tongue. Thus it will come about that Scripture will obtain a just authority among us, nor will anything happen to hinder us from blessing God, as in the whole course of his governance of the universe he deserves. But the petition is directed also to this end: that all impiety which has besmirched his holy name may perish and be wiped out; that all detractions and mockeries which dim this hallowing or diminish it may be banished; and that in silencing all sacrileges, God may shine forth more and more in his majesty.

The second petition

The second petition is: that God's Kingdom come. Even though it contains nothing new, it is with good reason kept separate from the first petition; for if we consider our languor in the greatest matters of all, we ought to extend our discussion in order to drive home something that ought to have been thoroughly known of itself. Therefore, after we have been bidden to ask God to subject and finally completely destroy everything that casts a stain upon his holy name, there is now added another similar and almost identical entreaty: that "his Kingdom come".

But even though the definition of this Kingdom was put before us previously, I now briefly repeat it: God reigns where men, both by denial of themselves and by contempt of the world and of earthly life, pledge themselves to his righteousness in order to aspire to a heavenly life. Thus there are two parts to this Kingdom: first, that God by the power of his Spirit correct all the desires of the flesh which by squadrons war against him; second, that he shape all our thoughts in obedience to his rule.

Therefore, no others keep a lawful order in this petition but those who begin with themselves, that is, to be cleansed of all corruptions that disturb the peaceful state of God's Kingdom and sully its purity. Now, because the word of God is like a royal sceptre, we are bidden here to entreat him to bring all men's minds and hearts into voluntary obedience to it. This happens when he manifests the working of his word through the secret inspiration of his Spirit in order that it may stand forth in the degree of honour that it deserves. Afterward we should descend to the impious, who stubbornly and with desperate madness resist his authority. Therefore God sets up his Kingdom by humbling the whole world, but in different ways. For he tames the wantonness of some, breaks the untameable pride of others. We must daily desire that God gather churches unto himself from all parts of the earth; that he spread and increase them in number; that he adorn them with gifts; that he establish a lawful order among them; on the other hand, that he cast down all enemies of pure teaching and religion; that he scatter their counsels and crush their efforts. From this it appears that zeal for daily progress is not enjoined upon us in vain, for it never goes so well with human affairs that the filthiness of vices is shaken and washed away, and full integrity flowers and grows. But its fullness is delayed to the final coming of Christ when, as Paul teaches, "God will be all in all".

Thus this prayer ought to draw us back from worldly corruptions, which so separate us from God that his Kingdom does not thrive within us. At the same time it ought to kindle zeal for mortification of the flesh; finally, it ought to instruct us in bearing the cross. For it is in this way that God wills to spread his Kingdom. But we should not take it ill that the outward man is in decay, provided the inner man is renewed! For this is the condition of God's Kingdom: that while we submit to his righteousness, he makes us sharers in his glory. This comes to pass when, with ever-increasing splendour, he displays his light and truth, by which the darkness and falsehoods of Satan's kingdom vanish, are extinguished, and pass away. Meanwhile, he protects his own, guides them by the help of his Spirit into uprightness, and strengthens them to perseverance. But he overthrows the wicked conspiracies of enemies, unravels their stratagems and deceits, opposes their malice, represses their obstinacy, until at last he slays Antichrist with the Spirit of his mouth, and destroys all ungodliness by the brightness of his coming.

The third petition

The third petition is: that God's will may be done on earth as in heaven. Even though it depends upon his Kingdom and cannot be separated from it, still it is with reason added separately on account of our ignorance, which does not easily or immediately comprehend what it means that God reigns in the world. It will therefore not be absurd to take it as an explanation that God will be King in the world when all submit to his will.

Here it is not a question of his secret will, by which he controls all things and directs them to their end. For even though Satan and men violently rebel against him, he knows that by his incomprehensible plan he not only turns aside their attacks but so orders it that he may do through them what he has decreed.

But here God's other will is to be noted—namely, that to which voluntary obedience corresponds—and for that reason, heaven is by name compared to earth, for the angels, as is said in the psalm, willingly obey God, and are intent upon carrying out his commands [Ps 103:20]. We are therefore bidden to desire that, just as in heaven nothing is done apart from God's good pleasure, and the angels dwell together in all peace and uprightness, the earth be in like manner subject to such a rule, with all arrogance and wickedness brought to an end.

And in asking this we renounce the desires of our flesh; for whoever does not resign and submit his feelings to God opposes as much as he can God's will, since only what is corrupt comes forth from us. And again by this prayer we are formed to self-denial so God may rule us according to his decision. And not this alone but also so he may create new minds and hearts in us, ours having been reduced to nothing in order for us to feel in ourselves no prompting of desire but pure agreement with his will. In sum, so we may wish nothing from ourselves but his Spirit may govern our hearts; and while the Spirit is inwardly teaching us we may learn to love the things that please him and to hate those which displease him. In consequence, our wish is that he may render futile and of no account whatever feelings are incompatible with his will.

Conclusion of the first part

Here, then, are the first three sections of the prayer. In making these requests we are to keep God's glory alone before our eyes, while leaving ourselves out of consideration and not looking to any advantage for ourselves; for such advantage, even though it amply accrues from such a prayer, must not be sought by us here. But even though all these things must nonetheless come to pass in their time, without any thought or desire or petition of ours, still we ought to desire and request them. And it is of no slight value for us to do this. Thus, we may testify and profess ourselves servants and children of God, zealously, truly, and deeply committed, to the best of our ability, to his honour. This we owe our Lord and Father, therefore, men who do not, with this desire and zeal to further God's glory, pray that "God's name be hallowed", that "his Kingdom come", that "his will be done", should not be reckoned among God's children and servants; and inasmuch as all these things will come to pass even against such men's consent, the result will be their confusion and destruction.

Exposition of the last three petitions

The fourth petition

The second part of the prayer follows, in which we descend to our own affairs. We do not, indeed, bid farewell to God's glory, which as Paul testifies is to be seen even in food and drink, and ask only what is expedient for us. But we have pointed out that there is this difference: God specifically claims the first three petitions and draws us wholly to himself to prove our piety in this way. Then he allows us to look after our own interests, yet under this limitation: that we seek nothing for ourselves without the intention that whatever benefits he confers upon us may show forth his glory, for nothing is more fitting than that we live and die to him.

But by this petition we ask of God all things in general that our bodies have need to use under the elements of this world, not only for food and clothing but also for everything God perceives to be beneficial to us, that we may eat our daily bread in peace. Briefly, by this we give ourselves over to his care, and entrust ourselves to his providence, that he may feed, nourish, and preserve us. For our most gracious Father does not disdain to take even our bodies under his safekeeping and guardianship in order to exercise our faith in these small matters, while we expect everything from him, even to a crumb of bread and a drop of water. For since it has come about in some way or other through our wickedness that we are affected and tormented with greater concern for body than for soul, many who venture to entrust the soul to God are still troubled about the flesh, still worry about what they shall eat, what they shall wear, and unless they have on hand abundance of wine, grain, and oil, tremble with apprehension. So much more does the shadow of this fleeting life mean to us than that everlasting immortality.

Those who, relying upon God, have once for all cast out that anxiety about the care of the flesh, immediately expect from him greater things, even salvation and eternal life. It is, then, no light exercise of faith for us to hope for those things from God which otherwise cause us such anxiety. And we benefit greatly when we put off this faithlessness, which clings to the very bones of almost all men.

What certain writers say in philosophizing about "super-substantial bread" seems to me to agree very little with Christ's meaning; indeed, if we did not even in this fleeting life accord to God the office of nourisher, this would be an imperfect prayer. The reason they give is too profane: that it is not fitting that children of God, who ought to be spiritual, not only give their attention to earthly cares but also involve God in these with themselves. As if his blessing and fatherly favour are not shown even in food, or it were written to no purpose that "godliness holds promise not only for the life to come but also for the present life" [1 Tim 4:8]. Now even though forgiveness of sins is far more important than bodily nourishment, Christ placed the inferior thing first that he might bring us gradually to the two remaining petitions, which properly belong to the heavenly life. In this he has taken account of our slowness.

But we are bidden to ask our daily bread that we may be content with the measure that our Heavenly Father has deigned to distribute to us, and not get gain by unlawful devices. Meanwhile, we must hold that it is made ours by title of gift; for, as is said in Moses, neither effort nor toil, nor our hands, acquire anything for us by themselves but by God's blessing [Deut 8:17-18]. Indeed, not even an abundance of bread would benefit us in the slightest unless it were divinely turned into nourishment. Accordingly, this generosity of God is necessary no less for the rich than for the poor; for with full cellars and storehouses, men would faint with thirst and hunger unless they enjoyed their bread through his grace.

The word "today", or "day by day", as it is in the other Evangelist, as well as the adjective "daily", bridle the uncontrolled desire for fleeting things, with which we commonly burn without measure, and to which other evils are added. For if a greater abundance is at hand, we vainly pour it out upon pleasure, delights, ostentation, and other sorts of excess. Therefore we are bidden to ask only as much as is sufficient for our need from day to day, with this assurance: that as our Heavenly Father nourishes us today, he will not fail us tomorrow. Thus, however abundantly goods may flow to us, even when our storehouses are stuffed and our cellars full, we ought always to ask for our daily bread, for we must surely count all possessions nothing except in so far as the Lord, having poured out his blessing, makes it fruitful with continuing increase. Also, what is in our hand is not even ours except in so far as he bestows each little portion upon us hour by hour, and allows us to use it. Because the pride of man only most grudgingly allows itself to be persuaded, the Lord declares that he provided a singular proof for every age when he fed his people in the desert with manna in order to impress upon us that man does not live by bread alone but rather by the word that proceeds out of his mouth. By this he shows it is by his power alone that life and strength are sustained, even though he administers it to us by physical means. So he commonly teaches us by the opposite example when he breaks, as often as he pleases, the strength of bread (and as he himself says, the Staff) that those who eat may waste away with hunger and those who drink may be parched with thirst.

Yet those who, not content with daily bread but panting after countless things with unbridled desire, or sated with their abundance, or carefree in their piled-up riches, beseech God with this prayer are but mocking him. For the first ones ask him what they do not wish to receive, indeed, what they utterly detest, namely, mere daily bread—and as much as possible cover up before God their propensity to greed, while true prayer ought to pour out before him the whole mind itself and whatever lies hidden within. But others ask of him what they least expect, that is, what they think they have within themselves.

In calling the bread "ours", God's generosity, as we have said, stands forth the more, for it makes ours what is by no right owed to us. Yet the point I also have touched upon must not be rejected: that what has been obtained by just and harmless toil is so designated, not what is got by frauds or robberies; for all that we acquire through harming another belongs to another.

The fact that we ask that it be given us signifies that it is a simple and free gift of God, however it may come to us, even when it would seem to have been obtained from our own skill and diligence, and supplied by our own hands. For it is by his blessing alone that our labours truly prosper.

The fifth petition

Next follows: "Forgive us our debts". With this and the following petition, Christ briefly embraces all that makes for the heavenly life, as the spiritual covenant that God has made for the salvation of his church rests on these two members alone: "I shall write my laws upon their hearts", and, "I shall be merciful toward their iniquity" [Jer 31:33; cf. 33:8]. Here Christ begins with forgiveness of sins, then presently adds the second grace: that God protect us by the power of his Spirit and sustain us by his aid so we may stand unvanquished against all temptations.

He calls sins "debts" because we owe penalty for them, and we could in no way satisfy it unless we were released by this forgiveness. This pardon comes of his free mercy, by which he himself generously wipes out these debts, exacting no payment from us but making satisfaction to himself by his own mercy in Christ, who once for all gave himself as a ransom. Therefore those who trust that God is satisfied with their own or others' merits, and that by such satisfaction forgiveness of sins is paid for and purchased, share not at all in this free gift. And while they call upon God according to this form, they do nothing but subscribe to their own accusation, and even seal their condemnation by their own testimony. For they confess they are debtors unless they are released by the benefit of forgiveness, which they still do not accept but rather spurn, while they thrust their merits and satisfactions upon God. For thus they do not entreat his mercy but call his judgement.

Let those who imagine such perfection for themselves as would make it unnecessary to seek pardon have disciples whose itching ears mislead them into errors, provided it be understood that all the disciples they acquire have been snatched away from Christ, seeing that in instructing all to confess their guilt, he admits none, but sinners; not that he would foster sins by flattery, but because he knew that believers are never divested of the vices of their flesh without always remaining liable to God's judgement. We must, indeed, wish and also zealously labour that, having discharged every detail of our duty, we may truly congratulate ourselves before God as being pure from every stain. But because it pleases God gradually to restore his image in us, in such a manner that some taint always remains in our flesh, it was most necessary to provide a remedy. But if Christ, according to the authority given him by his Father, commands us throughout life to resort to prayer for the pardon of our guilt, who will tolerate these new doctors, who try to dazzle the eyes of the simple-minded with the spectre of perfect innocence so as to assure them that they can rid themselves of all blame? This, according to John, is nothing else than to make God a liar!

Also, with the same effort these rascals, by cancelling one section of it, tear apart God's covenant, in which we see our salvation contained, and topple it from its foundation. Not only are they guilty of sacrilege in separating things till now joined, but also they are impious and cruel in overwhelming miserable souls with despair. Indeed, they are faithless to themselves and those like them because they induce a state of indolence diametrically opposed to God's mercy. But their objection, that in longing for the coming of God's Kingdom we at the same time seek the abolition of sin, is very childish. For in the first section of the prayer, the highest perfection is set before us, but in the latter, our weakness. Thus these two admirably accord with each other, so that, in aspiring toward the goal, we may not neglect the remedies that our necessity requires.

"As we forgive …"

Finally, we petition that forgiveness come to us, "as we forgive our debtors": namely, as we spare and pardon all who have in any way injured us, either treating us unjustly in deed or insulting us in word. Not that it is ours to forgive the guilt of transgression or offence, for this belongs to God alone! This, rather, is our forgiveness: willingly to cast from the mind wrath, hatred, desire for revenge, and willingly to banish to oblivion the remembrance of injustice. For this reason, we ought not to seek forgiveness of sins from God unless we ourselves also forgive the offences against us of all those who do or have done us ill. If we retain feelings of hatred in our hearts, if we plot revenge and ponder any occasion to cause harm, and even if we do not try to get back into our enemies' good graces, by every sort of good office deserve well of them, and commend ourselves to them, by this prayer we entreat God not to forgive our sins. For we ask that he do to us as we do to others. This, indeed, is to petition him not to do it to us unless we ourselves do it. What do people of this sort gain from their petition but a heavier judgement?

Finally, we must note that this condition—that he "forgive us as we forgive our debtors"—is not added because by the forgiveness we grant to others we deserve his forgiveness, as if this indicated the cause of it. Rather, by this word the Lord intended partly to comfort the weakness of our faith. For he has added this as a sign to assure us he has granted forgiveness of sins to us just as surely as we are aware of having forgiven others, provided our hearts have been emptied and purged of all hatred, envy, and vengeance. Also, it is partly by this mark that the Lord excludes from the number of his children those persons who, being eager for revenge and slow to forgive, practise persistent enmity and foster against others the very indignation that they pray to be averted from themselves. This the Lord does that such men dare not call upon him as Father. This is also eloquently expressed in Luke, in Christ's words.

The sixth petition
The sixth petition, as we have said, corresponds to the

promise that the law is to be engraved upon our hearts, but because we obey God not without continual warfare and hard and trying struggles, here we seek to be equipped with such armour and defended with such protection that we may be able to win the victory. By this we are instructed that we need not only the grace of the Spirit, to soften our hearts within and to bend and direct them to obey God, but also his aid, to render us invincible against both all the stratagems and all the violent assaults of Satan. Now the forms of temptations are indeed many and varied. For wicked conceptions of the mind, provoking us to transgress the law, which either our own inordinate desire suggests to us or the devil prompts, are temptations, as are things not evil of their own nature yet which become temptations through the devil's devices, when they are so thrust before our eyes that by their appearance we are drawn away or turn aside from God. And these temptations are either from the right or from the left. From the right are, for example, riches, power, honours, which often dull men's keenness of sight by the glitter and seeming goodness they display, and allure with their attractions, so that, captivated by such tricks and drunk with such sweetness, men forget their God. From the left are, for example, poverty, disgrace, contempt, afflictions, and the like. Thwarted by the hardship and difficulty of these, they become despondent in mind, cast away assurance and hope, and are at last completely estranged from God.

We pray God, our Father, not to let us yield to the two sorts of temptations which, either aroused in us by our inordinate desire or proposed to us by the devil's guile, war against us. We pray, rather, that he sustain and encourage us by his hand so that, strengthened by his power, we may stand firm against all the assaults of our evil enemy, whatever thoughts he may introduce into our minds. Then we pray that whatever is presented to us tending either way we may turn to good—namely, that we may not be puffed up in prosperity or yet cast down in adversity.

Nevertheless, we do not here ask that we feel no temptations at all, for we need, rather, to be aroused, pricked, and urged by them, lest, with too much inactivity, we grow sluggish. For it is not beside the point that David wished to be tempted and it is not without cause that the Lord daily tests his elect, chastising them by disgrace, poverty, tribulation, and other sorts of affliction. But God tries in one way, Satan in another. Satan tempts that he may destroy, condemn, confound, cast down; God so that by proving his own children he may make trial of their sincerity, and establish their strength by exercising it. Thus he may mortify, purify, and cauterise their flesh, which unless it were forced under this restraint would play the wanton and boast beyond measure. Besides, Satan attacks those who are unarmed and unprepared that he may crush them unaware. God, along with the temptation, makes a way of escape, that his own may be able patiently to bear all that he imposes upon them.

It makes very little difference whether we understand by the word 'evil' the devil or sin. Indeed, Satan himself is the enemy who lies in wait for our life; moreover, he is armed with sin to destroy us. This, then, is our plea: that we may not be vanquished or overwhelmed by any temptations but may stand fast by the Lord's power against all hostile powers that attack us. This is not to succumb to temptations that, received into his care and safekeeping and secure in his protection, we may victoriously endure sin, death, the gates of hell, and the devil's whole kingdom. This is to be freed from evil.

Here we must carefully note that it is not in our power to engage that great warrior the devil in combat, or to bear his force and onslaught. Otherwise it would be pointless or a mockery to ask of God what we already have in ourselves. Obviously those who prepare for such a combat with self-assurance do not sufficiently understand with what a ferocious and well-equipped enemy they have to deal. Now we seek to be freed from his power, as from the jaws of a mad and raging lion; if the Lord did not snatch us from the midst of death, we could not help being immediately torn to pieces by his fangs and claws, and swallowed down his throat. Yet we know that if the Lord be with us, and fight for us while we keep still, in his might we shall do mightily. Let others trust as they will in their own capacities and powers of free choice, which they seem to themselves to possess. For us let it be enough that we stand and are strong in God's power alone.

But this prayer involves more than at first sight it presents. For if God's Spirit is our power to battle with Satan, we shall never be able to win victory until, filled with the Spirit, we cast off all weakness of our flesh. While we petition, then, to be freed from Satan and sin, we anticipate that new increases of God's grace will continually be showered upon us, until, completely filled therewith, we triumph over all evil.

To some it seems rough and harsh to ask God not to lead us into temptation, seeing that to tempt us is against his nature, as James so testifies [Jas 1:13]. But the question has already been partly solved, because our lust is properly the cause of all temptations that vanquish us, and therefore bears the blame. And James means only that it is futile and unjust to transfer to God those vices which we are compelled to impute to ourselves because we know ourselves to be guilty of them. But this does not prevent God, when it seems good to him, from turning us over to Satan, from casting us into a reprobate mind and foul desires, and from leading us into temptations, by a just but often secret judgement. For the cause has often been hidden from men, while it is certain with him. From this we gather it is not an improper expression, if we are convinced that with good reason he threatens so many times to give sure proofs of his vengeance, when he strikes the reprobate with blindness and hardness of heart.

The conclusion

These three petitions, in which we especially commend to God ourselves and all our possessions, clearly show what we have previously said: that the prayers of Christians ought to be public, and to look to the public edification of the church and the advancement of the believers' fellowship. For each man does not pray that something be given to him privately, but all of us in common ask our bread, forgiveness of sins, not to be led into temptation, and to be freed from evil.

Moreover, there is added the reason why we should be so bold to ask and so confident of receiving. Even though this is not extant in the Latin versions, it is so appropriate to this place that it ought not to be omitted—namely, that his "is the Kingdom, and the power, and the glory, forever". This is firm and tranquil repose for our faith. For if our prayers were to be commended to God by our worth, who would dare even mutter in his presence? Now, however miserable we may be, though unworthiest of all, however devoid of all commendation, we will yet never lack a reason to pray, never have our assurance taken from us, since his Kingdom, power, and glory can never be snatched away from our Father.

At the end is added, "Amen". By it is expressed the warmth

of desire to obtain what we have asked of God. And our hope is strengthened that all things of this sort have already been brought to pass, and will surely be granted to us, since they have been promised by God, who cannot deceive. And this agrees with the form of prayer we previously set forth: "Do, O Lord, for thy name's sake, not on account of us or our righteousness". By this the saints not only express the end of their prayers but confess themselves unworthy to obtain it unless God seeks the reason from himself, and that their confidence of being heard stems solely from God's nature.

Concluding considerations:
adequacy of the Lord's Prayer, with freedom to use other words
The Lord's Prayer as a binding rule

We have everything we ought, or are at all able, to seek of God, set forth in this form and, as it were, rule for prayer handed down by our best Master, Christ, whom the Father has appointed our teacher and to whom alone he would have us hearken. For he both has always been the eternal Wisdom of God and, made man, has been given to men, the angel of great counsel.

And this prayer is in all respects so perfect that any extraneous or alien thing added to it, which cannot be related to it, is impious and unworthy to be approved by God. For in this summary he has set forth what is worthy of him, acceptable to him, necessary for us—in effect, what he would willingly grant.

For this reason, those who dare go farther and ask anything from God beyond this: first, wish to add to God's wisdom from their own, which cannot happen without insane blasphemy; secondly, do not confine themselves within God's will but, holding it in contempt, stray away farther in their uncontrolled desire; lastly, they will never obtain anything, since they pray without faith. But doubtless all such prayers are made apart from faith, for here the word of God is absent, upon which faith, if it is to stand at all, must always rely. But those who, neglecting the Master's rule, give themselves over to their own desires not only lack God's word but contend against it with all their strength. Therefore Tertullian has both truly and elegantly called it "the lawful prayer", tacitly indicating that all other prayers lie outside the law and are forbidden.

The Lord's Prayer does not bind us to its form of words but to its content

We would not have it understood that we are so bound by this form of prayer that we are not allowed to change it in either word or syllable. For here and there in Scripture one reads many prayers, far different from it in words, yet composed by the same Spirit, the use of which is very profitable to us. Many prayers are repeatedly suggested to believers by the same Spirit, which bear little similarity in wording. In so teaching, we mean only this: that no man should ask for, expect, or demand, anything at all except what is included, by way of summary, in this prayer; and though the words may be utterly different, yet the sense ought not to vary. Thus all prayers contained in Scripture, and those which come forth from godly breasts, are certainly to be referred to it. Truly, no other can ever be found that equals this in perfection, much less surpasses it. Here nothing is left out that ought to be thought of in the praises of God, nothing that ought to come into man's mind for his own welfare. And, indeed, it is so precisely framed that hope of attempting anything better is rightly taken away from all men. To sum up, let us remember that this is the teaching of Divine Wisdom, teaching what it willed and willing what was needful.

Special times of prayer and undiscouraged perseverance in it
Prayer at regular times
But, although it has already been stated above that, lifting up our hearts, we should ever aspire to God and pray without ceasing, still, since our weakness is such that it has to be supported by many aids, and our sluggishness such that it needs to be goaded, it is fitting each one of us should set apart certain hours for this exercise. Those hours should not pass without prayer, and during them all the devotion of the heart should be completely engaged in it. These are: when we arise in the morning, before we begin daily work, when we sit down to a meal, when by God's blessing we have eaten, when we are getting ready to retire.

But this must not be any superstitious observance of hours, whereby, as if paying our debt to God, we imagine ourselves paid up for the remaining hours. Rather, it must be a tutelage for our weakness, which should be thus exercised and repeatedly stimulated. We must take particular care that, whenever we either are pressed or see others pressed by any adversity, we hasten back to God, not with swift feet but with eager hearts. Also, that we should not let our prosperity or that of others go unnoticed, failing to testify, by praise and thanksgiving, that we recognize God's hand therein.

Lastly, in all prayer we ought carefully to observe that our intention is not to bind God to particular circumstances, or to prescribe at what time, in what place, or in what way he is to do anything. Accordingly, in this prayer we are taught not to make any law for him, or impose any condition upon him, but to leave to his decision to do what he is to do, in what way, at what time, and in what place it seems good to him. Therefore, before we make any prayer for ourselves, we pray that his will be done. By these words we subject our will to his in order that, restrained as by a bridle, it may not presume to control God but may make him the arbiter and director of all its entreaties.

Patient perseverance in prayer
If, with minds composed to this obedience, we allow ourselves to be ruled by the laws of divine providence, we shall easily learn to persevere in prayer and, with desires suspended, patiently to wait for the Lord. Then we shall be sure that, even though he does not appear, he is always present to us, and will in his own time declare how he has never had ears deaf to the prayers that in men's eyes he seems to have neglected. This, then, will be an ever-present consolation: that, if God should not respond to our first requests, we may not faint or fall into despair. Such is the inclination of those who, carried away with their own zeal, so call upon God that unless he attends upon their first act of prayer and brings them help at once, they immediately fancy him angry and hostile toward them and, abandoning all hope of being heard, cease to call upon him. Rather, by deferring our hope with a well-tempered evenness of mind, let us follow hard upon that perseverance which Scripture strongly commends to us. For in the Psalms we can often see that David and other believers, when they are almost worn out with praying and seem to have beaten the air with their prayers as if pouring forth words to a deaf God, still do not cease to pray. For, unless the faith placed in it is superior to all events, the authority of God's Word does not prevail.

Also, let us not tempt God and, wearying him with our

depravity, provoke him against ourselves. This is usual with many who covenant with God only under certain conditions, and, as if he were the servant of their own appetites, bind him to laws of their own stipulation. If he does not obey them at once, they become indignant, grumble, protest, murmur, and rage at him. To such, therefore, he often grants in wrath and fury what in mercy he denies to others to whom he is favourable. The children of Israel supply proof of this, for whom it would have been much better not to be heard by the Lord than to swallow his wrath with their meat.

Unheard prayers?

But if finally even after long waiting our senses cannot learn the benefit received from prayer, or perceive any fruit from it, still our faith will make us sure of what cannot be perceived by sense, that we have obtained what was expedient. For the Lord so often and so certainly promises to care for us in our troubles, when they have once been laid upon his bosom. And so he will cause us to possess abundance in poverty, and comfort in affliction. For though all things fail us, yet God will never forsake us, who cannot disappoint the expectation and patience of his people. He alone will be for us in place of all things, since all good things are contained in him and he will reveal them to us on the Day of Judgement, when his Kingdom will be plainly manifested.

Besides, even if God grants our prayer, he does not always respond to the exact form of our request but, seeming to hold us in suspense, he yet, in a marvellous manner, shows us our prayers have not been vain. This is what John's words mean: "If we know that he hears us whenever we ask anything of him, we know that we have obtained the requests we asked of him" [1 John 5:15]. This seems an excess of words, but the declaration is especially useful because God, even when he does not comply with our wishes, is still attentive and kindly to our prayers, so that hope relying upon his word will never disappoint us. But believers need to be sustained by this patience, since they would not long stand unless they relied upon it. For the Lord proves his people by no light trials, and does not softly exercise them, but often drives them to extremity, and allows them, so driven, to lie a long time in the mire before he gives them any taste of his sweetness. And, as Hannah says, "He kills and brings to life; he brings down to hell and brings back" [1 Sam 2:6]. What could they do here but be discouraged and rush into despair if they were not, when afflicted, desolate, and already half dead, revived by the thought that God has regard for them and will bring an end to their present misfortunes? Nevertheless, however they stand upon the assurance of that hope, they do not meanwhile cease to pray, for unless there be in prayer a constancy to persevere, we pray in vain.

CRANMER ON SALVATION

King Henry VIII is famous for creating the Church of England, but it was men like Thomas Cranmer who made it Protestant in doctrine. Cranmer was Archbishop of Canterbury during the crucial years of the Reformation in sixteenth-century England, and was a key player in the liturgical and theological reform of the period. Cranmer had become convinced that the gospel rediscovered and expounded by Martin Luther was the true biblical gospel. Salvation was in Christ alone, through faith alone, by grace alone, and taught in Scripture alone.

On the basis of this growing conviction, Cranmer drafted much of the Anglican *Book of Common Prayer* and the *Thirty-Nine Articles*, and gave to both their thoroughly Reformed Protestant character. In these two documents, Cranmer was to have a profound and lasting influence on the English-speaking church, not only in his lifetime, but for centuries to come.

The three homilies ('homily' is simply another word for 'sermon') included below were written as expositions of the biblical gospel of Christ. They functioned not only as sermons to be read by clergy not learned enough to compose their own, but also as doctrinal statements for the English church as to what constituted true biblical Christianity. The first homily explains justification by faith alone; the second what true faith is; and the third what true and godly works are. Although the content is weighty, the tone is warm and pastoral. These are sermons addressed to the people.

We cannot prove that Cranmer actually wrote these three homilies, as his name did not originally appear on them. However, scholars of the period agree that they came from his pen, based on internal evidence as well as the fact that other writers at the time asserted that Cranmer was the author. The text presented here is taken from the Parker Society edition of 1846; the English has been updated to make reading easier.

Homily of salvation
by Thomas Cranmer

ecause all are sinners and offenders against God, and breakers of his law and commandments, no-one by his own acts, works, and deeds (no matter how good they seem) can be justified and made righteous before God. It is necessary for everyone to seek for another righteousness, or justification, to be received from God's own hands; that is to say, the remission, pardon, and forgiveness of his sins and trespasses for whatever things he has done. And this justification or righteousness, which we receive by God's mercy and Christ's merits, embraced by faith, is taken, accepted, and allowed by God for our perfect and full justification.

So that we may understand this more fully, it is our part and duty always to remember the great mercy of God. We remember that (when all the world was wrapped in sin by breaking of the law) God sent his only Son our Saviour Christ into this world, to fulfil the law for us. By shedding his most precious blood, he made a sacrifice and satisfaction, or (as it may be called) amends to his Father for our sins, to appease his wrath and indignation against us for those sins. We are brought to God's favour, and made his children and inheritors of his kingdom of heaven. Those who sin, when they convert and sincerely turn again to God, are washed from their sins by this sacrifice, in such a way that there remains no spot of sin that will count towards their damnation. This is the justification or righteousness which Paul speaks of, when he says: "No man is justified by the works of the law, but freely by faith in Jesus Christ". And again he says: "We believe in Christ Jesus, that we are justified freely by the faith of Christ, and not by the works of the law, because no man will be justified by the works of the law".

Although this justification is free to us, yet it does not come so freely that there is no ransom paid at all.

But here some may be bewildered, reasoning in this way: if a ransom is paid for our redemption, then it is not given to us freely. A prisoner who pays his ransom is not let go freely—if he goes freely, then he goes without ransom. For what else is it to go freely, than to be set at liberty without payment of a ransom? This reasoning is satisfied by the great wisdom of God in the mystery of our redemption. He has so combined his justice and mercy together, that he would neither satisfy his justice by condemning us to the perpetual captivity of the devil, and his prison of hell, without remedy for ever, without mercy; nor satisfy his mercy by delivering us clearly, without justice, or payment of a just ransom. He joined his most upright and equal justice with his endless mercy. That is, he showed his great mercy to us in delivering us from our former captivity, without requiring any ransom to be paid by us, or amends to be made upon our parts (which was impossible for us to do). Because it was not within our capacity to do it, he provided a ransom for us. That was the most precious body and blood of his most dear and best beloved son Jesus Christ, who, besides his ransom, fulfilled the law for us perfectly.

And so the justice of God and his mercy embraced together, and fulfilled the mystery of our redemption. Paul speaks of this justice and mercy of God knit together in the third chapter to the Romans: "All have sinned and fall short of the glory of God, and are justified freely by his grace through the redemption that came by Christ Jesus. God presented him as a sacrifice of atonement, through faith in his blood. He did this to demonstrate his justice." And in the tenth chapter: "Christ is the end of the law so that there may be righteousness for everyone who believes". And in the eighth chapter: "What the law was powerless to do in that it was weakened by the sinful nature, God did by sending his own Son in the likeness of sinful man to be a sin offering. And so he condemned sin in sinful man, in order that the righteous requirements of the law might be fully met in us, who do not live according to the sinful nature but according to the Spirit."

In these places the apostle touches especially on three things, which must concur and go together in our justification. Upon God's part it is great mercy and grace. Upon Christ's part, it is justice—that is, the satisfaction of God's justice, the price of our redemption, by the offering of his body and shedding of his blood, and fulfilling the law perfectly and thoroughly. Upon our part, it is true and lively faith in the merits of Jesus Christ—which even so is not ours, but comes through God's work in us.

So in our justification is not only God's mercy and grace, but also his justice. It consists of paying our ransom, and fulfilling the law. So the grace of God does not exclude the justice of God in our justification, but only excludes the justice of man—that is to say, the justice of our works as merits deserving our justification. Therefore Paul declares here that nothing is required upon the behalf of man concerning his justification, but only a true and lively faith; which nevertheless is the gift of God, and not man's only work without God.

Yet faith does not exclude repentance, hope, love, dread, and the fear of God, which are to be joined with faith in every man that is justified. It does exclude them from the role of justifying; so that although they are all present together in him that is justified, yet they do not all justify. Faith also does not exclude the requirement of our good works, which are necessary to be done because of duty towards God (for we are obliged to serve God in doing good deeds, commanded by him in his holy Scripture, all the days of our life). But it does exclude them, in that we may not do them in order to be made good by doing them. All the good works that we can do are imperfect, and therefore are not able to deserve our justification. Our justification comes freely by the mere mercy of God, and of such great and free mercy, that although all the world was not able of themselves to pay any part towards their ransom, it pleased our heavenly Father, because of his infinite mercy, without our desert or deserving, to prepare for us the most precious jewels of Christ's body and blood. By them our ransom is fully paid, the law fulfilled, and his justice fully satisfied. So Christ is now the righteousness of all those who truly believe in him. He paid their ransom for them by his death; and he fulfilled the law for them in his life. Now in him, and by him, every true Christian may be called a fulfiller of the law—for that which their infirmity lacked, Christ's justice supplied.

The second part of the sermon of salvation

You have heard who it is from whom all men ought to seek their justification and righteousness, and how also this righteousness comes by Christ's death and merits. You heard also that three things are required for the obtaining of our righteousness: that is, God's mercy, Christ's justice, and a true and lively faith. Out of this faith springs good works.

Before it was declared that no-one can be justified by his own good works, because no-one fulfils the law, according to the full requirements of the law. Paul, in his epistle to the Galatians, proves this, saying "If a law had been given that could impart life, then righteousness would certainly have come by the law". And again he says: "If righteousness could be gained through the law, Christ died for nothing". And again he says: "You who are trying to be justified by law have fallen away from grace". And furthermore he writes to the Ephesians this: "By grace you have been saved, through faith, and this not from yourselves, it is the gift of God, not by works, so that no-one can boast". To be short, the sum of all Paul's argument is this: that if justice comes from works, then it does not come from grace; and if it comes from grace, then it does not come from works. All the prophets reach this conclusion, as Peter says in the tenth chapter of Acts: "All the prophets testify about him that everyone who believes in him receives forgiveness of sins through his name".

All the old and ancient authors speak of being justified in this way, by this true and lively faith in Christ—both Greeks and Latins. I will especially write of three: Hilary, Basil, and Ambrose. Hilary says these words plainly in the ninth canon upon Matthew: "Only faith justifies". Basil, a Greek author, writes "This is a perfect and a complete glorifying in God, when a man does not boast in himself for his own justice, but knows himself certainly to be unworthy of true justice, and to be justified by faith in Christ alone. This is a perfect and a complete rejoicing in God, when a man does not put himself forward for his own righteousness, but acknowledges himself to lack true justice and righteousness, and to be justified by faith in Christ alone. And Paul", says Basil, "glories in the worthlessness of his own righteousness, and looks for his righteousness from God by faith."

These are the very words of Basil. Ambrose, a Latin author, says these words: "This is the ordinance of God, that he who believes in Christ should be saved without works, by faith alone, freely receiving remission of his sins". Consider diligently these words "without works", "by faith alone", "freely we receive remission of our sins". What can be spoken more plainly than to say that, freely, without works, by faith only, we obtain remission of our sins? We often read these and other similar sentences—that we are justified by faith only, freely, and without works—in the best and most ancient writers. Besides Hilary, Basil, and Ambrose, mentioned above, we read the same in Origen, Chrysostom, Cyprian, Augustine, Prosper, Oecumenuis Photius, Bernardus, Anselm, and many other authors, Greek and Latin.[5]

Nevertheless, they do not mean by this sentence (that we are "justified by faith only") that justifying faith is alone in man, without true repentance, hope, charity, dread, and the fear of God, at any time or season. Nor when they say that we are justified freely, do they mean that we should or might be idle afterwards, and that nothing will be required on our part afterwards. They do not mean that because we are justified without our good works, we should do no good works at all. More of this will be expressed later. But this proposition, that we are justified by faith alone, freely, and without works, is spoken to take away all merit of our works, as being insufficient to deserve our justification from God's hands. It thereby expresses most plainly the weakness of man, and the goodness of God. It expresses our great infir-

5. Cranmer needed to quote ancient authors to demonstrate that the doctrines of the Reformation (accused of being new and radical innovations) were actually a return to ancient Christianity.

mity, and the might and power of God; the imperfection of our own works, and the most abundant grace of our Saviour Christ. It thereby wholly ascribes the merit and deserving of our justification to Christ alone, and his most precious blood-shedding. The holy Scripture teaches this faith; this is the strong rock and foundation of Christian religion. This doctrine is approved by all old and ancient authors of Christ's church. This doctrine advances and sets forth the true glory of Christ, and suppresses the vain-glory of man. Whoever denies it is not to be thought of as a true Christian man, nor as a setter-forth of Christ's glory, but an adversary of Christ and his gospel, and a setter-forth of men's vain-glory.

Although this doctrine is so true (as it is most true indeed), that we are justified freely, without any merit of our own good works (as Paul expresses it), and freely, by this lively and perfect faith in Christ only, as the ancient authors use to speak it—yet this true doctrine must also be truly understood, and plainly declared, so that carnal men will not use it wrongly to live carnally according to the appetite and will of the world, the flesh, and the devil. So that no man will err by mistaking this doctrine, I will plainly and briefly declare the right understanding of this, so that no man can truly think that he may use it for carnal liberty to follow the desires of the flesh. You must not think that any kind of sin can be committed, or any ungodly living followed.

First, you must understand that justification by Christ is not a combination of the work of God to man, and the work of man to God. Justification is not the work of man, but of God. Man cannot justify himself by his own works, neither in part, nor in the whole. To affirm that a man might by his own works take away and purge his own sins, and so justify himself, would be the greatest arrogance and presumption of man that antichrist could erect against God. Justification is the office of God alone, and is not a thing which we offer to him, but which we receive from him. It is not something we give to him, but which we take from him, by his free mercy, and by the merits of his most dearly-beloved Son, our only Redeemer, Saviour, and Justifier, Jesus Christ. So the true understanding of this doctrine is not that our own act of believing in Christ, or our faith in Christ which is within us, justifies us, and merits our justification to us. That would be to consider ourselves to be justified by some act or virtue that is within ourselves. But the true understanding and meaning of it is, that although we carry God's word, and believe it; although we have faith, hope, charity, repentance, dread, and fear of God within us, and do ever so many good works because of it; yet we must renounce the merit of all our virtues, of faith, hope, charity, and all our other virtues and good deeds, which we either have done, shall do, or can do. These are things far too weak and insufficient and imperfect to deserve remission of our sins, and our justification. Therefore we must trust only in God's mercy, and in that sacrifice which our High Priest and Saviour Christ Jesus, the Son of God, once offered for us upon the cross. We thereby obtain God's grace and remission both of our original sin in baptism, and all actual sin committed by us after our baptism, if we truly repent and genuinely convert to him again. We should be like John the Baptist, who although he was so virtuous and godly a man, yet in this matter of forgiving of sin he turned the people away from himself. He instead pointed them to Christ, saying to them, "Behold, there is the Lamb of God, who takes away the sins of the world". As great and godly a virtue as lively faith is, yet it turns us from itself, and sends or points us to Christ, so we will have only him for our remission of our sins, or justification. So our faith in Christ (as it were) says to us: It is not I who takes away your sins, but it is Christ only; and to him alone I send you for that purpose, renouncing all your good virtues, words, thoughts, and works, and only putting your trust in Christ.

The third part of the sermon of salvation

It has been openly declared to you that no-one can fulfil the law of God, and therefore all are condemned by the law. It followed necessarily that some other thing should be required for our salvation than the law. That thing is a true and a lively faith in Christ, which brings forth good works, and a life according to God's commandments. You also heard the ancient authors' minds on this, saying that faith in Christ alone justifies man, so plainly declared that you see the very true meaning of this proposition.

Thus you see that the very true sense of this proposition (we are justified by faith in Christ alone), according to the old ancient authors, is this: we put our faith in Christ, so that we will be justified by him alone, that we are justified by God's free mercy, and the merits of our Saviour Christ alone. It is by no virtue or good work of our own that is in us, or that we are able to have or to do to deserve it. Christ himself is the only cause deserving it.

Here you see many words are used to avoid contention with those who delight to brawl about words, and also to show the true meaning, to avoid mistake and misunderstanding. Yet perhaps even this will not serve for those who are contentious, for contenders will always forge a matter of contention, even when they have no basis to do so. Notwithstanding, we continue so that the rest may profit—those who are more desirous to know the truth (when it is plain enough) than to contend about it, and to obscure and darken it with argumentative and petty quibbles.

It is true that our own works do not justify us. That is to say, our works do not merit or deserve remission of our sins and make us, the unjust, just before God. But God out of his mere mercy, through the merits and deservings of his Son Jesus Christ, justifies us. Nevertheless, because faith sends us directly to Christ for remission of our sins, and by faith from God we embrace the promise of God's mercy and of the remission of our sins (something none of our virtues or works properly do), therefore Scripture often says that faith without works does justify. Therefore the ancient fathers of the church from time to time have spoken of our justification by saying "faith alone justifies us". By this they mean nothing other than what Paul meant, when he said faith without works justifies us. And because all of it is brought to pass through the merits and deservings of our Saviour Christ alone (and not through our merits, or through the merit of any virtue that we have within us or of any work that comes through the merit and deserving) we renounce altogether, as it were, faith, works, and all other virtues. For our own imperfection is so great, through the corruption of original sin, that all that is within us is imperfect. This includes faith, love, hope, dread, thoughts, words and works. These things, therefore, are not worthy to merit and deserve any part of our justification for us. And we use this form of speaking, when we humble ourselves to God, to give all the glory to our Saviour Christ, who is most worthy to have it.

Here you have heard the work of God in our justification, and how we receive it from him freely, by his mercy, without our deserts, through true and lively faith. Now you shall hear the work and duty of a Christian to God—what we ought on our part to render to God for his great mercy and goodness. Our obligation is not to pass the time of this present life unfruitfully and idly (after we are baptized or justified), not caring how few good works we do to the glory of God, and to the profit of our neighbours. Much less is it our duty, after we are made members of Christ, to live contrary to that— making ourselves members of the devil, walking according to his enticements, and the suggestions of the world and the flesh. By such actions we know that we serve the world and the devil, and not God.

For that faith which brings forth (without repentance) either evil works, or no good works, is not a right, pure, and lively faith, but a dead, devilish, counterfeit, and pretend faith, as Paul and James call it. Even the devils know and believe that Christ was born of a virgin; that he fasted forty days and forty nights without meat and drink; that he did all kind of miracles, declaring himself God. They also believe that Christ for our sakes suffered a most painful death, to redeem us from eternal death, and that he rose again from death on the third day. They believe that he ascended into heaven, and that he sits on the right hand of the Father, and at the end of this world shall come again, and judge both the living and the dead. The devils believe these articles of our faith. They believe all things that are written in the New and Old Testaments to be true. Yet despite all this faith they are still devils, remaining in their damnable state, lacking the true Christian faith.

For the right and true Christian faith is, not only to believe that holy Scripture and all the articles of our faith mentioned above are true, but also to have a sure trust and confidence in God's merciful promises. This is to be saved from everlasting damnation by Christ, from which follows a loving heart to obey his commandments. No devil has this true Christian faith. Nor does any man who in the outward profession of his mouth, and in his outward receiving of the sacraments, in coming to the church, and in all other outward appearances, seems to be a Christian, and yet in his living and deeds shows the contrary. For how can a man have this true faith, this sure trust and confidence in God, that by the merits of Christ his sins are remitted, and he is reconciled to the favour of God, and to be partaker of the kingdom of heaven by Christ—when he lives in an ungodly way, and denies Christ in his deeds? Surely no such ungodly person can have this faith and trust in God. For as they know Christ to be the only Saviour of the world, so they know also that the wicked shall not possess the kingdom of God. They know that God hates unrighteousness; that he will destroy all those who speak falsely. They know that those who have done good works (which cannot be done without a lively faith in Christ) shall come into the resurrection of life, and those that have done evil shall come to the resurrection of judgement. And they know very well also that to those who are contentious, and to those who will not be obedient to the truth, but will obey unrighteousness, will come indignation, wrath and affliction.

Therefore, to conclude, considering the infinite benefits of God, shown and exhibited to us mercifully without our deserts—God who has not only created us from nothing, and from a piece of vile clay by his infinite goodness—God has exalted us, our souls, to be in his own similitude and likeness. Also, although we were condemned to hell and death eternal, he has given his own natural Son, who was God, immortal, and equal to himself in power and glory. He gave him to be incarnate, and to take our mortal nature upon him, with its infirmities, and in the same nature to suffer a most shameful and painful death for our offences, to justify us and to restore us to life everlasting. In doing this he made us also his dear beloved children, brothers to his only Son our Saviour Christ, and inheritors forever with him of his eternal kingdom of heaven. These great and merciful benefits from God, if they are considered well, neither give us reason to be idle, and to live without doing any good works, nor by any means stir us up to do evil things. On the contrary, if we are not desperate persons with hearts harder than stones, they move us to give ourselves wholly to God, with all our will, hearts, might, and power, to serve him in all good deeds, obeying his commandments during our lives. They tell us to seek in all things his glory and honour, not our sensual pleasures and vain glory; evermore dreading to offend such a merciful God and loving Redeemer, in word, thought or deed. These benefits from God, deeply considered, move us for his sake also always to be ready to give ourselves to our neighbours, and, as much as it lies with us, to study with all our endeavour to do good to every man. These are the fruits of the true faith: to do good, as much as it lies in us, to every man, and above all things, and in all things, to advance the glory of God. From him alone have we our sanctification, justification, salvation and redemption, to whom be ever glory, praise, and honour, world without end. Amen.

A short declaration of the true, lively and Christian faith

by Thomas Cranmer

The first entry to God, good Christian people, is through faith, by which (as it was declared in the last sermon) we are justified before God. So that no-one should be deceived for lack of right understanding of this, you must note diligently that faith is taken in the Scripture in two ways. There is one faith which in Scripture is called a dead faith, which brings forth no good works, but is idle, barren and unfruitful. The holy apostle James compares this faith to the faith of devils, who believe God to be true and just, and tremble for fear, yet they do nothing well, but all evil. This is the faith of the wicked and ungodly Christian people who confess God (as Paul says) with their mouth, but deny him in their deeds, and are abominable, and without the right faith, and in all good works reprehensible. This faith is a persuasion and belief in man's heart, which means that he knows that there is a God, and assents to all truth of God's most holy word, contained in holy Scripture, but it consists only in believing that the word of God is true. This is not properly called faith.

Someone who reads the works of Caesar, believing them to be true, has a knowledge of Caesar's life and noble acts because he believes the history of Caesar. Yet it is not that he believes in Caesar, from whom he expects no help nor benefit. It is the same with someone who believes that all that is spoken of God in the Bible is true, and yet lives in such an ungodly way that he cannot expect to enjoy the promises and benefits of God. It may be said that such a man has a faith and belief in the words of God. Yet it is not really true that he believes in God, or has a faith and trust in God by which he may expect grace, mercy, and eternal life at God's hand. Rather, he may expect indignation and punishment, according to the merits of his wicked life. For, as it is written in a book said to be by Didymus Alexandrinus: "Inasmuch as faith without works is dead, it is not truly faith, as a dead man is not a man". This dead faith, therefore, is not that sure and substantial faith which saves sinners.

There is another faith in Scripture, which is not idle, unfruitful, and dead like the previous faith. It works by love as Paul declares (Gal 5). As the other, false faith is called a dead faith, so may this be called a living faith. This is not only belief in the doctrines of our faith, but it is also a sure trust and confidence in the mercy of God through our Lord Jesus Christ. It is a steadfast hope of all good things to be received from God's hand. It trusts that, although through weakness or temptation by our spiritual enemy we fall from him by sin, yet if we return to him with true repentance, he will forgive and forget our offences for his Son's sake, our Saviour Jesus Christ. He will even make us inheritors with him of his everlasting kingdom. In the meantime, until that kingdom comes, he will be our protector and defender in all perils and dangers, whatever may happen. Though sometimes he sends us sharp adversity, yet he will always be a loving father to us, correcting us for our sin, but not withdrawing his mercy from us. So we must trust in him and commit ourselves wholly to him, hang only upon him, and call upon him, ready to obey and serve him.

This is the true, lively, and unfeigned Christian faith. It is not in the mouth and outward profession only, but it lives and stirs inwardly in the heart. This faith does not exist without hope and trust in God, nor without the love of God and of our neighbours. It does not exist without fear of God, nor without the desire to hear God's word, and to follow it in avoiding evil and doing all good works gladly. This faith, as Paul describes it, is "being sure of what we hope for and certain of what we do not see". And later he says "anyone who comes to God must believe that he exists and that he rewards those who earnestly seek him".[6] And nothing commends good men to God so much as this assured faith and trust in him.

Three things should be especially noted about this faith. First, this faith does not lie dead in the heart, but is lively and fruitful in bringing forth good works. Second, without it no good works can be done that will be acceptable and pleasant to God. Third, we should note what kind of good works this faith brings forth.

For the first: just as light cannot be hidden, but will show itself at one place or another, so true faith cannot be kept secret. When opportunity is offered, it will break out and show itself by good works. The living body of a man always does things appropriate to a natural and living body, for nourishment and preservation of itself, as it has need, opportunity, and occasion. In the same way the soul which has a living faith in it will always be doing some good work, which declares that it is living. It will not be unoccupied.

6. Heb 11:1, 6. Cranmer considered Paul the author of the book of Hebrews.

Therefore, when men hear in the Scriptures such high commendations of faith—that it makes us please God, live with God, and to be the children of God—if then they imagine that they are set at liberty from doing all good works, and may live as they please, they trifle with God, and deceive themselves. It is a manifest sign that they are far from having the true and living faith, and also far from knowledge of what true faith means. For the true, sure and living Christian faith (as said before) is not just to believe all things about God which are contained in holy Scripture, but it is also an earnest trust and confidence in God. It is trusting that he cares for us and looks after us, as the father of a child whom he loves. It is knowing that he will be merciful to us for his only Son's sake, and that we have our Saviour Christ as our perpetual advocate and priest. In his merits, sacrifice, and suffering, we trust that our offences are continually washed and purged, whenever we repent truly, and return to him with our whole heart. At the same time we are steadfastly determined to obey and serve him in keeping his commandments (through his grace), and never to turn back again to sin.

Such is the true faith that Scripture commends so much. Such faith, when it considers what God has done for us, is also moved, through continual assistance of the Spirit of God, to serve and please him. It is moved to keep his favour, to fear his displeasure, to continue his obedient children, showing thankfulness by observing his commandments. It does it freely, primarily out of true love and not for dread of punishment or love of temporal reward, knowing how much, without deserving it, we have received his mercy and pardon freely.

This true faith will show itself, and cannot be idle for long. As it is written, "The righteous man will live by faith".

He neither sleeps, nor is idle, when he should wake and be well occupied. God says by his prophet Jeremiah: "Blessed is the man who trusts in the Lord, whose confidence is in him. He will be like a tree planted by the water that sends out its roots by the stream. It does not fear when heat comes; its leaves are always green. It has no worries in a year of drought and never fails to bear fruit". In the same way, those who are faithful and put away their fear of adversity will show the fruit of their good works, as opportunity is offered to do them.

The second part of the sermon of faith

You have heard in the first part of this sermon that there are two kinds of faith: a dead and unfruitful faith, and a living faith that works by love. The first is unprofitable; the second is necessary for obtaining our salvation. This faith always has love joined to it, and is fruitful, bringing forth all good works. Now more follows concerning this matter.

The wise man says: "He who believes in God will listen to his commandments". For if we do not show ourselves faithful in our actions, the faith which we pretend to have is only a feigned faith. The true Christian faith is clearly shown by good living, and not by words alone. As Augustine says, "Good living cannot be separated from true faith, which works by love". And Chrysostom says: "Faith by itself is full of good works: as soon as a man believes, he will be decorated with them".

How many good works will be found in this faith, and how it makes one man's work more acceptable to God than another man's, Paul teaches at some length in the eleventh chapter to the Hebrews. He says that faith made the offering of Abel better than the offering of Cain. It made Noah build the ark. It made Abraham leave his country, and all his friends, and go into a far country, to dwell among strangers. So did Isaac and Jacob, depending only on the help and trust that they had in God. And when they came to the country which God promised them, they did not build cities, towns, or houses, but lived like strangers in tents that could be moved. Their trust was so much in God that they set little importance in any worldly thing. God had prepared for them better dwelling-places in heaven, of his own foundation and building.

This faith made Abraham ready at God's command to offer his own son and heir Isaac, whom he loved so much, and by whom he was promised to have innumerable offspring. What is more, among these offspring one would be born through whom all nations would be blessed. Yet Abraham trusted so much in God that he believed that even if his son was slain, God would be able by his omnipotent power to raise him from death, and carry out his promise. He did not doubt the promise of God, although to his reason everything seemed against it. He believed truly that God would not forsake him in the famine that was in the country. And in all other dangers that came upon him, he always trusted that God would be his God and his protector, whatever he saw to the contrary.

This faith worked so much in the heart of Moses that he refused to be taken as Pharaoh's daughter's son, and have a great inheritance in Egypt. He thought it better to have affliction and sorrow with the people of God, than to live pleasantly for a time with evil men in sin. By faith he did not care about Pharaoh's threats. His trust was so much in God that he did not think about the happiness of this world, but looked for the reward to come in heaven. He set his heart upon the invisible God, as if he always saw him present before his eyes.

By faith the children of Israel passed through the Red Sea. By faith the walls of Jericho fell down without a stroke, and many other wonderful miracles were done. In all good men that have lived, faith has brought forth their good works and obtained the promises of God. Faith has stopped the lions' mouths. Faith has quenched the force of fire. Faith has escaped the sword's edges. Faith has given weak men strength, victory in battle, overthrown the armies of infidels and raised the dead to life. Faith has made good men take adversity well. Some have been mocked and whipped, bound and cast in prison; some have lost all their goods, and lived in great poverty; some have wandered in mountains, hills, and wilderness. Some have been racked, some slain, some stoned, some sawn, some rent in pieces, some beheaded, some tortured without mercy and refused to be delivered, because they looked to rise again to a better state.

All these fathers, martyrs, and other holy men, of whom Paul spoke, had their faith surely fixed in God when all the world was against them. They did not only know God to be Lord, maker and governor of all people in the world, but also had a special confidence and trust that he was and would be their God—their comforter, aider, helper, maintainer and defender. This is the Christian faith, which these holy men had, and we also ought to have. Although they were not called Christians, it was still a Christian faith that they had. They looked for all benefits from God the Father through the merits of his Son Jesus Christ, as we now do. There is one difference between them and us: they looked for when Christ would come, and we are in the time when he has come. Therefore Augustine says: "The time has changed, but not the faith". For we both have one faith in one Christ. Furthermore, as Paul says, they had the same Holy Spirit that we have. For as the Holy Spirit teaches us to trust in God, and to call upon him as our Father, so did he teach them to say (as it is written) "you, O Lord, are our Father, our Redeemer from of old is your name". God gave them grace to be his children, as he does for us now. But now, because of the coming of our Saviour Christ, we have received the Spirit of God more abundantly in our hearts. By it we can have a greater faith, and a surer trust, than many of them had. But, in effect, we and they are all one. We have the same faith that they had in God, and they the same that we have. Paul praises their faith so much because, now that Christ has come, we should give ourselves wholly to Christ in profession and living more, not less, than the old fathers did before his coming. By all the declarations of Paul it is evident that the true, lively and Christian faith is not a dead, vain or unfruitful thing. Rather, it is a thing of perfect virtue, of wonderful working and strength, bringing forth all good actions and good works.

All holy Scripture bears witness and agrees that a true and lively faith in Christ brings forth good works. Therefore every man must examine himself diligently to know whether he has the same true lively faith in his heart, or not. He will know this by the fruits. Many who professed the faith of Christ erred in that they thought they knew God and believed in him, when in their life they declared to the contrary. John in his first Epistle refutes this error: "We know that we have come to know him if we obey his commands. The man who says, 'I know him', but does not do what he commands, is a liar, and the truth is not in him". Again he says: "No-one who continues to sin has either seen him or known him. Dear children, do not let anyone lead you astray." And moreover he says: "This then is how we know that we belong to the truth, and how we set our hearts at rest in his presence whenever our hearts condemn us. For God is greater than our hearts, and he knows everything. Dear friends, if our hearts do not condemn us, we have confidence before God and receive from him anything we ask, because we obey his commands and do what pleases him". And still further he says: "Everyone who believes that Jesus is the Christ is born of God ... and we know that anyone born of God does not continue to sin; the one who was born of God keeps him safe, and the evil one cannot harm him". And finally he concludes, showing the cause why he wrote this Epistle, saying: "I write these things to you who believe in the name of the Son of God so that you may know that you have eternal life". In his third Epistle he confirms the whole matter of faith and works in a few words, saying: "Anyone who does what is good is from God. Anyone who does what is evil has not seen God."

As John says, the living knowledge and faith of God brings forth works. He says the same about hope and love, that they cannot stand with evil. Of hope he writes: "We know that when God appears, we shall be like him, for we shall see him as he is. Everyone who has this hope in him purifies himself, just as he is pure." Of love he says these words: "If anyone obeys his word, God's love is truly made complete in him". Again he says: "This is love for God: to obey his commands". John did not write this as a clever idea of his own devising, but as a most certain and necessary truth, taught to him by Christ himself. For Christ is the eternal and infallible Truth, who in many places clearly affirms that faith, hope, and love cannot be without good and godly works.

John says concerning faith, "He who has the Son has life; he who does not have the Son of God does not have life". He confirms this with a double oath, saying "Truly, truly, I say to you, he who believes in me has everlasting life". Now, if he who believes in Christ has everlasting life, it must follow that he who has this faith must also have good works, and be studious to observe God's commandments obediently. For those who have evil works and lead their life in disobedience and transgression of God's commandments, without repentance, do not have everlasting life, but everlasting death. As Christ himself says, "Those who do evil will go away to eternal punishment, but the righteous to eternal life". Again he says: "I am the Alpha and the Omega, the Beginning and the End. To him who is thirsty I will give to drink without cost from the spring of the water of life. He who overcomes will inherit all this, and I will be his God and he will be my son. But the cowardly, the unbelieving, the vile, the murderers, the sexually immoral, those who practise magic arts, the idolaters and all liars—their place will be in the fiery lake of burning sulphur. This is the second death." Just as Christ undoubtedly affirms that true faith brings forth good works, he says likewise of love: "Whoever has my commands and obeys them, he is the one who loves me". He also says: "If anyone loves me, he will obey my teaching ... he who does not love me will not obey my teaching". And as the love of God is proved by good works, so is the fear of God also. As the wise man says, "The fear of God puts away sin", and also: "He who fears God will do good works".

The third part of the sermon of faith

You have heard in the second part of this sermon that no man should think that he has the living faith which Scripture commands, if he does not live obediently to God's laws. All good works spring out of that faith. Also it has been demonstrated to you by examples that faith makes men steadfast, quiet and patient in all affliction. Now concerning the same matter, more follows.

A man can easily deceive himself and think in his own imagination that he knows God by faith, loves him, fears him, and belongs to him, when in fact he does nothing of the sort. The test of all these things is a very godly and Christian life. He who sets his heart to seek God's honour, and studies to know the will and commandments of God, and to conform himself to them—such a man rejoices in God. He who does not follow the desire of his own flesh to serve the devil by sin, but sets his mind to serve God, for God's own sake—he perceives by his own life that he truly has a right knowledge of God. He who for God's sake sets himself to love all his neighbours, whether they are friends or adversaries, doing good to every man as opportunity arises and willingly hurting no man—he has a lively faith, a constant hope, a true and genuine love and fear of God. But some cast away the yoke of God's commandments from their necks, and give themselves to live without true repentance according to their own sensual minds and pleasures. They disregard God's word and much less live according to it. Such people clearly deceive themselves, and do not see their own hearts, if they think that they either know God, love him, fear him, or trust him.

Some, perhaps, imagine that they belong to God, although they live in sin. They come to the church, and present themselves as God's dear children. But John says plainly: "If we claim to have fellowship with him yet walk in the darkness, we lie and do not live by the truth." Others vainly think that they know and love God, although they do not obey his commandments. But John says clearly: "The man who says,

'I know him', but does not do what he commands, is a liar". Some falsely persuade themselves that they love God, when they hate their neighbours. But John says clearly: "If anyone says, 'I love God', yet hates his brother, he is a liar", and "Anyone who claims to be in the light but hates his brother is still in the darkness. Whoever loves his brother lives in the light, and there is nothing in him to make him stumble. But whoever hates his brother is in the darkness and walks around in the darkness; he does not know where he is going, because the darkness has blinded him." And moreover he says: "This is how we know who the children of God are and who the children of the devil are: Anyone who does not do what is right is not a child of God; nor is anyone who does not love his brother".

Therefore do not deceive yourselves, thinking that you have faith in God, or that you love God, or trust in him, or fear him, when you live in sin. Your ungodly and sinful life declares the contrary, whatever you say or think. It is necessary for a Christian man to have this true Christian faith, and to test himself as to whether he has it or not. He needs to know what belongs to it, and how it works in him. It is not the world that we can trust—the world, and all in it, is vanity. It is God who must be our defence and protection against all temptations of wickedness and sin, errors, superstition, idolatry and all evil. If all the world was on our side, and God against us, how much could the world do? Therefore let us set our whole faith and trust in God, and neither the world, the devil nor all their power can prevail against us.

Let us therefore, good Christian people, try to examine our faith. Let us not flatter ourselves but examine our works, and so judge what our faith is. Christ himself speaks of this matter, and says: "Each tree is recognized by its own fruit".

Therefore let us do good works, and so declare our faith to be living Christian faith. Let us show our election to be sure and stable by the virtues which ought to spring out of faith. As Peter teaches: "be all the more eager to make your calling and election sure". He also says: "Add to your faith goodness; and to goodness, knowledge; and to knowledge, self-control; and to self-control, perseverance; and to perseverance, godliness; and to godliness, brotherly kindness; and to brotherly kindness, love". In this way we will show indeed that we have true living Christian faith, and so we may both comfort our conscience that we are in right faith, and also by these means comfort other men.

If these fruits do not follow, we mock God, deceive ourselves, and also other men. We may bear the name of Christian men, but we lack the true faith that belongs to that name. For true faith always brings forth good works. As James says, show your faith by your deeds. Your deeds and works must be an open testimonial of your faith. Otherwise your faith, being without good works, is only the devils' faith, the faith of the wicked, an imaginary faith and not a true Christian faith. The devils and evil people are no better off for their counterfeit faith, but it in fact adds to the cause of their damnation. There are those who are christened, and have received knowledge of God and of Christ's merits, and yet live idly on purpose, without good works. They think the mere name of faith is enough for them, or else, setting their minds upon vain pleasures of this world, live in sin, without repentance. They do not bear the fruits that belong to such a noble name. Upon such presumptuous persons and wilful sinners must remain the great vengeance of God and eternal punishment in hell, prepared for the devil and wicked people.

Therefore, as you profess the name of Christ, good Christian people, let no such fantasy and imagination of faith deceive you at any time. Be sure of your faith, test it by your living, and examine the fruits that come from it. Take notice of the increase of love and charity towards God and your neighbour that it brings. In this way you will see it to be a true, living faith. If you feel and perceive such a faith in you, rejoice in it, and be diligent to maintain it, and keep it in yourself. Let it increase daily, and work more and more, and you can be sure that you will please God by this faith. In the end, when it is God's will, you will come to him and receive "the goal of your faith, the salvation of your souls" (as Peter names it), as other faithful men have done before. God, who has promised it to his faithful people, will grant this to us! To God be all honour and glory, world without end. Amen.

Homily or sermon of good works joined to faith

by Thomas Cranmer

In the last sermon, it was described to you what the living and true faith of a Christian is. It does not cause a man to be idle, but to be occupied in bringing forth good works, as the occasion demands.

Now, by God's grace, the second thing that was noted before will be demonstrated. That is, without faith no work can be done which is pleasant and acceptable to God. "No branch can bear fruit by itself; it must remain in the vine", said our saviour Christ. "Neither can you bear fruit unless you remain in me. I am the vine; you are the branches. If a man remains in me and I in him, he will bear much fruit; apart from me you can do nothing." Paul says that Enoch had faith, because he pleased God. "Without faith", Paul says, "it is impossible to please God". He also said to the Romans, "Everything that does not come from faith is sin".

Faith gives life to the soul. Those who lack faith are as much dead to God as those whose bodies lack breath are to the world. Without faith all that we do is dead before God, no matter how bright and glorious the work seems before man. An engraved or painted picture is just a dead representation of the thing itself, and is without life or any kind of movement. Such are the works of all unfaithful persons before God. They appear to be living works, but indeed they are dead, doing nothing in regards to eternal life. They are shadows and shows of living and good things, and not good and living things themselves. For true faith gives life to the works, and out of such faith comes good works, that are in truth good works. Without it, no work is good before God.

Augustine said, "We must not put good works before faith, nor think that before faith a man can do any good work. Such works, although they seem to men to be praiseworthy, are in fact in vain, and not allowed before God. They are like the course of a horse that runs astray; it takes a great deal of effort, but to no purpose. Let no man, therefore", he said, "depend upon his good works before his faith. If faith is not there, neither are good works. The intent", says he, "makes the works good; but faith must guide and order the intentions of man." Christ says: "If your eyes are bad, your whole body will be full of darkness".

"The eye signifies the intent", says Augustine, "by which a man does something. So if someone does not do his good works with a godly intent, and a true faith that works by love, then his whole body—that is to say, the whole amount of his works—is dark and there is no light in it." Good deeds are not measured and discerned from vices by the facts themselves, but by the ends and intents for which they are done. If a heathen man clothes the naked, feeds the hungry and does other such works, even so because he does not do them in faith for the honour and love of God, they are dead, vain, and fruitless works for him. It is faith that commends the work to God. "For", as Augustine says, "whether you want it so or not, the work that does not come from faith is worthless".

Where faith in Christ is not the foundation, there is no good work, no matter what building we make. "There is one work, in which are found all good works, that is faith which works by charity". If you have that, you have the basis of all good works; for the virtues of strength, wisdom, temperance, and justice, all depend upon this same faith. Without this faith we do not have them, but only their names and shadows. As Augustine says: "The whole life of those who lack true faith is sin. Nothing is good without him who is the author of goodness. Where he is not, there is only feigned virtue—even though it might be in the best works." And Augustine, in explaining this verse of the psalm—"The turtle has found a nest where she may keep her young birds"—says that Jews, heretics and pagans do good works; they clothe the naked, feed the poor, and do other good works of mercy. But because they are not done in the true faith, the birds are lost. But if they remain in faith, then faith is the nest and safeguard of their birds. That is to say, faith is the safeguard of their good works, so that their reward is not utterly lost.

This matter (which Augustine argues in many books) Ambrose concludes in a few words, saying "He who would by nature withstand vice—either by natural will or reason—spends the time of this life in vain, and does not reach true virtues. For without worshipping the true God, that which seems to be virtue is vice."

The most plain writer to this purpose is John Chrysostom, who writes: "You will find many who do not have the true faith, and are not of the flock of Christ, and yet (it seems) they grow in good works of mercy. You will find them full of pity, compassion, and devoted to justice. Yet for all that, they have no fruit from their works, because the chief work is lacking. For when the Jews asked Christ what they should do to work good works, he answered: 'The work of God is this: to believe in the one he has sent'. He called faith the work of God. As soon as a man has faith, then he grows in good works. For faith of itself is full of good works, and nothing is good without faith." As an illustration, he said that "those who glisten and shine in good works without faith in God, are like dead men who have beautiful and precious tombs, and yet it does not help them at all. Faith may not be naked without works, for then it is no true faith. When it is joined to works, it is still above the works. As bodies first have life, and then are nourished, so must our faith in Christ come first, and then be nourished with good works. Life may be without nourishment, but nourishment cannot be without life. A man must be nourished by good works, but first he must have faith. He who does good deeds without faith does not have life. I can show a man who lived by faith without works, and still came to heaven; but without faith no man had life at all. The thief who was hanged when Christ suffered only believed, and the most merciful God justified him. You may object that he lacked time to do good works, and otherwise he would have done them. That is true, and I will not contend with you. But I will surely affirm that faith alone saved him. If he had lived, and ignored faith and its works, he would have lost his salvation again. But I say that faith by itself saved him, while works by themselves never justified any man." Having heard the mind of Chrysostom you may perceive that faith is not without works (if you have the opportunity for them) and works cannot gain eternal life without faith.

The second part of the sermon of good works
In the former sermon three things were especially noted about faith, and you have had two described to you. The first was that faith is never idle or without good works, when there is opportunity. The second is that good works acceptable to God cannot be done without faith.

Now to proceed to the third thing which was noted in the former sermon about faith. That is, what kind of works spring out of true faith, and lead faithful men to eternal life? No-one can know this as well as our Saviour Christ himself. A certain great man asked him the question: "What good thing must I do to get eternal life?" Jesus answered: "If you want to enter life, obey the commandments". But the prince, not satisfied with this, asked further: "Which ones?" The scribes and Pharisees had made so many of their own laws and traditions to bring men to heaven, apart from God's commandments, that this man was in doubt whether he should come to heaven by those laws and traditions, or by the laws of God. Therefore he asked Christ which commandments he meant. Christ made him a plain answer, repeating the commandments of God, saying: "Do not murder, do not commit adultery, do not steal, do not give false testimony, honour your father and mother, and love your neighbour as yourself". By these words Christ declared that the laws of God are the way that leads to eternal life, and not the traditions and laws of men. This is to be taken as a true lesson taught by Christ's own mouth. The works of the moral commandments of God are the true works of faith, which lead to the blessed life to come.

But the blindness and malice of man, even from the beginning, has always been ready to fall from God's commandments. Adam the first man, who only had the one commandment that he should not eat of the forbidden fruit, despite God's commandment blamed the woman, who was seduced by the subtle persuasion of the serpent, and so followed his own will, and left God's commandment. Ever since that time his descendants have been so blinded by original sin, that they have always been ready to turn away from God and his law, and to invent a new way to salvation by works of their own device. Almost all the world has forsaken the true honour of the only eternal living God, and wandered about with their own fantasies. Some worship the sun, the moon, or the stars; some Jupiter, Juno, Diana, Saturn, Apollo, Neptune, Ceres, Bacchus, and other dead men and women. Some, not satisfied with that, worshipped diverse kinds of beasts, birds, fish, fowl and serpents. Every region, town and house was divided in this way and set up images of such things as they liked, and worshipped them. Such was the degradation of the people after they fell to their own fantasies, and left the eternal living God and his commandments, so that they devised innumerable images and gods. They remained in this error and blindness until the time when Almighty God, pitying the blindness of man, sent his true prophet Moses into the world, to condemn this extreme madness. He also came to teach the people to know the only living God, and his true honour and worship.

But the corrupt inclination of man was so much given to following his own fantasies, that all the admonitions, exhortations, promises and threatenings of God could not keep man from his inventions. Despite all the blessings of God shown to the people of Israel, when Moses went up into the mountain to speak with Almighty God, he had been there only a few days when the people began to invent new gods. It came into their heads to make a calf of gold, and they kneeled down and worshipped it. After that they followed the Moabites, and worshipped the Moabites' god. Read the book of Judges, the books of the Kings, and the Prophets; and there you will find how unfaithful the people were, how full of inventions and more keen to run after their own fantasies than God's most holy commandments. There you will read of

Baal, Moloch, Chamos, Mechom, Baalpeor, Astaroth, Bel the dragon, Priapus, the brass serpent, the twelve signs, and many others. The people invented pilgrimages to these images, decking them with precious jewels and kneeling down and offering to them. They thought this a high merit before God, to be esteemed above the laws and commandments of God. At that time God commanded sacrifices to be made only in Jerusalem. Yet they did totally the contrary, making altars and sacrifices everywhere, in hills, in woods, and in houses, not regarding God's commandments but thinking their own fantasies and devotion better than them.

This error was spread so far abroad that not only the ordinary people, but also the priests and teachers of the people were corrupted and blindly seduced with the same abominations, partly by glory and greed, and partly by ignorance. King Ahab's only true minister of God was Elijah, while eight hundred and fifty priests persuaded him to honour Baal, and to perform sacrifices in the woods or groves. This horrible error continued until the three noble kings, Jehoshaphat, Josiah, and Hezekiah, God's elect ministers, destroyed it and brought the people from their pretend inventions to the true commandments of God. For doing this, their immortal reward and glory remains with God for ever.

Furthermore, the inclination of man to have his own holy devotions led to new sects and religions, called Pharisees, Sadducees, and Scribes. They had many holy and godly traditions and laws (as it seemed by the outward appearance and bright glistening of their works) but indeed it all tended to idolatry, superstition and hypocrisy. For their hearts within were full of malice, pride, covetousness and iniquity. Against these sects, and their pretended holiness, Christ cried out more vehemently than he did against any other persons. He would say (and often repeated) these words: "Woe to you, teachers of the law and Pharisees, you hypocrites! You clean the outside of the cup and dish, but inside they are full of greed and self-indulgence. Blind Pharisee! First clean the inside of the cup and dish." They had all the godly traditions and outward shows of good works, devised by their own imagination, by which they appeared to the world most religious and holy of all men. But Christ, who saw their hearts, knew that they were inwardly, in the sight of God, the most unholy, most abominable and the furthest from God of all men. Therefore he said to them: "You nullify the word of God for the sake of your tradition. You hypocrites! Isaiah was right when he prophesied about you: 'These people honour me with their lips, but their hearts are far from me. They worship me in vain; their teachings are but rules taught by men.'"

Although Christ said that those who teach doctrines and commandments of men worship in vain, he did not mean to overthrow all men's commandments. He himself was always obedient to the princes and their laws, which were made for good order and government of the people. However, he reproved the laws and traditions made by the scribes and Pharisees. They were not made for the good order of the people (as the civil laws were), but were so highly extolled that they were made out to be a right and sincere way to worship God, as if they were equal with God's laws or above them. For many of God's laws could not be kept, but gave way to them. God detested this arrogance, that man would so advance his laws as to make them equal with God's laws. The true way of honouring and right way of worshipping God is in his laws, but they omitted his laws. God has appointed his laws by which his pleasure is to be honoured. It is also his pleasure that all man's laws, as long as they are not contrary to his laws, will be obeyed and kept, as good and necessary for every commonwealth—but not as things in which his honour principally rests. All civil laws, man's laws, are or should be made to induce men to observe God's laws better, so that consequently God will be honoured better because of them.

However, the scribes and Pharisees were not content that their laws should be honoured no more than other civil laws. Nor would they let them be called by the name of other temporal laws, but called them holy and godly traditions. They wanted them esteemed, not just as a right and true way to worship God (as God's laws are indeed) but also as the highest way of honouring God, to which the commandments of God should give way. This was the reason why Christ so vehemently spoke against them, saying that their traditions, which men esteemed so highly, were abominations before God. For commonly when such traditions abound, the transgression of God's commandments follows. Also people will have greater devotion in the observing of such traditions, and greater guilt for breaking them, than they have for the commandments of God.

The scribes and Pharisees, for instance, scrupulously kept the Sabbath, to the extent that they were offended with Christ because he healed sick men on that day, and with his apostles because they (being hungry) gathered ears of corn to eat on that day. Because his disciples did not wash their hands as often as the traditions required, the scribes and Pharisees quarrelled with Christ, saying: "Why do your disciples break the tradition of the elders?" But Christ retorted against them that they, in order to observe their own traditions, taught men to break the very commandments of God. They taught the people such a devotion that they offered their goods into the treasure-house of the temple (under the pretence of God's honour), leaving their fathers and mothers, to whom they were most importantly bound, without help. In this way they broke the commandments of God to keep their own traditions. They esteemed an oath made by the gold or offering in the temple more than an oath made in the name of God himself, or of the temple itself. They were more studious to pay their tithes of small things, than to do the greater things commanded of God (such as works of mercy, or to do justice, or to deal sincerely, uprightly, and faithfully with God and man). "You should have practised the latter", said Christ, "without neglecting the former". To be short, they had such blind judgement that they stumbled over a straw, and leaped over a block. They would nicely take a fly out of their cup, as it were, and drink down a whole camel. Therefore Christ called them "blind guides", warning his disciples from time to time to reject their doctrine. To the world they seemed to be perfect men, both in life and teaching. But their lives were just hypocrisy and their doctrine sour leaven, mixed with superstition, idolatry and preposterous judgement. They set up the traditions and ordinances of man in the place of God's commandments.

The third part of the sermon of good works

In the second part of this sermon it has been demonstrated what kind of good works God wants his people to walk in, so that all men might judge good works rightly. The works God desires are those he has commanded in his holy Scripture, and not such works as men have studied out of their own brain, out of a blind zeal and devotion, without the word of God. By mistaking the nature of good works, man has highly displeased God, and has departed from his will and commandment.

You have now heard how much the world, from the beginning until Christ's time, was always ready to fall from the commandments of God. People wished to seek other means to honour and serve him, following a devotion imagined out of their own heads. You have also heard how they extolled their own traditions as highly as (or above) God's commandments. This has happened in our times (the more it is to be lamented) no less than it did among the Jews. It has happened by the corruption, or at the least by the negligence, of those people who ought to have preferred God's commandments and to have preserved the sincere and heavenly doctrine left by Christ. What man, who has any judgement or learning, joined with a true zeal for God, does not see and lament to see such false doctrine, superstition, idolatry, hypocrisy, and other abuses entered into Christ's religion? To see, little by little, through the sour leaven of these things, that the sweet bread of God's holy word has been hindered and laid apart? Never in their greatest blindness did the Jews have so many pilgrimages to images and so much kneeling, kissing, and offering incense to them, as has been common in our time. There was not one fortieth the amount of sects and feigned religions among the Jews, and nor were they more superstitiously and ungodly abused than they have been among us of late. These sects and religions had so many hypocritical works in their state of religion, as they arrogantly named it, that their lamps (as they said) always ran over, able to provide satisfaction not only for their own sins but also for all their benefactors, brothers and sisters of their religion. In a most ungodly and crafty way they had persuaded the multitude of ignorant people, keeping in various places 'markets of merits', which were full of their holy relics, images, shrines, and works of supererogation, ready to be sold. All things which they had were called holy: holy cowls, holy girdles, holy pardoned beads, holy shoes, holy rules, and all full of holiness. What thing can be more foolish, more superstitious, or ungodly, than that men, women, and children, should wear a friar's coat to deliver them from fevers or pestilence? When they die, or when they are buried, they cause it to be cast on them, hoping thereby to be saved. This superstition, although thanks be to God it has been little used in this realm, has been and is still used among many people, both learned and unlearned.

But let us pass over the innumerable superstitions that people have had about strange apparel, silence, dormitory, cloister, chapter, choice of meats and drinks, and the like. Let us consider what abuses have been in the three chief principal points—which they called the three essentials of religion—that is to say, obedience, chastity, and wilful poverty.

First, under pretence of obedience to their father in religion (which obedience they invented themselves), they were exempted by their rules and canons from obedience to their natural father and mother. They were also exempted from obedience to emperor and king, and all temporal power, whom they were bound to obey out of duty to God's laws. And so their profession of obedience which was not due, was a renunciation of the obedience which was due. As to how their profession of chastity was observed, it is more decent to pass over this in silence, and let the world judge of that which is well known. This is better than to offend chaste and godly ears with unchaste words, by expressing their unchaste life. As for their wilful poverty, it was such that in possessions—jewels, plate, and riches—they were equal or above merchants, gentlemen, barons, earls and dukes. Yet by this subtle and dubious term, proprium in common (property in common), they deluded the world, persuading everyone that despite all their possessions and riches, they observed their vow, and were in fact living in wilful poverty. But for all their riches, they could not help father nor mother, nor any others who were indeed very needy and poor, without the permission of their father abbot, prior or warden. They might take from every man, but they could not give anything to any man, not even to those whom the laws of God bound them to help. And so, through their traditions and rules, the laws of God could not rule them. Therefore it might be truly said of them the same thing that Christ spoke to the Pharisees: "You nullify the word of God for the sake of your tradition; you honour God with your lips, but your hearts are far from him". The longer the prayers were that they used by day and by night, under pretence of holiness—to get the favour of widows and other simple folks, so that they might sing masses and services for their husbands and friends, and admit them into their prayers[7]—the more Christ's saying is true of them. "Woe to you, teachers of the law and Pharisees, you hypocrites! You devour widows' houses, under cover of long prayers; therefore your damnation will be the greater. Woe to you, teachers of the law and Pharisees, you hypocrites! You travel over land and sea to win a single convert, and when he becomes one, you make him twice as much a son of hell as you are."

Honour be to God, who put light in the heart of his faithful and true minister of most famous memory, King Henry the Eighth. God gave him knowledge of his word, and an earnest desire to seek his glory, and to put away all superstitious and pharisaical sects invented by antichrist. He led

7.   That is, be paid to say prayers for dead relatives.

him to set up again the true word of God, and the glory of his most blessed name, as he did the most noble and famous princes, Jehoshaphat, Josiah, and Hezekiah. God grant that we, the king's faithful and true subjects, might feed on the sweet and savoury bread of God's own word. May we, as Christ commanded, reject all the pharisaical and popish leaven of man's pretend religion. Although it is abominable before God, and contrary to God's commandments and Christ's pure religion, yet it was extolled to be a godly life and the highest state of perfection. As if a man might be more godly and more perfect by keeping the rules, traditions, and professions of men, than by keeping the holy commandments of God.

To pass over the ungodly and counterfeit religions, let us remember some other kinds of popish superstitions and abuses. They were things such as beads, lady psalters, rosaries, fifteen Oos, St Bernard's verses, St Agatha's letters, purgatory, satisfactory masses, stations and jubilees, feigned relics, hallowed beads, bells, bread, water, palms, candles, fire, and the like. Also superstitious fastings, fraternities, pardons, with such merchandise.[8] Such things were esteemed and abused (to the great prejudice of God's glory and commandments) so much that they were considered high and most holy things, by which to gain eternal life or remission of sin. Likewise, vain inventions, unfruitful ceremonies and ungodly laws,

8.   These are referring to medieval church practices which were meant to make a person more holy. The Fifteen Oos or Oes of St Bridget were prayers on the last words of Jesus. The eight verses of St Bernard from the Psalms were claimed to preserve from damnation anyone who said them every day. Agatha was a virgin martyr saint of early Roman Christianity, who was prayed to. Beads, bells and the other paraphernalia were part of religious ceremonies.

decrees, and councils of Rome, were so important that nothing was thought comparable in authority, wisdom, learning and godliness to them. The laws of Rome, they said, were to be received by all men as much as the laws of the four evangelists. All laws of princes must give way to them. And the laws of God were also partly omitted and esteemed less, so that the said laws, decrees, and councils, with their traditions and ceremonies, might be more duly observed and held in greater reverence. Thus the people were so blinded (through ignorance) with the bright show and appearance of those things, that they thought that observing them was more holy, a more perfect service and honouring of God, and more pleasing to God, than keeping God's commandments.

This has been the corrupt inclination of man—always tending to superstition, to make new ways of honouring God out of his own head, and then to have more affection and devotion to observe them, than to search out God's holy commandments and to keep them. Furthermore, men take God's commandments for men's commandments, and men's commandments for God's commandments, indeed for the highest and most perfect and holy of all God's commandments. All was so confused that only a few well-learned men, a small number at that, knew or at least wanted to know the truth, and dared to affirm the truth, to separate God's commandments from the commandments of men. And so grew much error, superstition, idolatry, vain religion, preposterous judgement and great contention, with all ungodly living.

So if you have any zeal for the right and pure honouring of God; if you have any regard for your own souls, and to the life that is to come, which is both without pain and without end; then apply yourselves above all things to read and to hear God's word. Mark in it diligently what his will is that you should do, and with all your endeavour apply your-selves to do it. First, you must have an assured faith in God, and give yourselves wholly to him. Love him in prosperity and adversity, and dread to offend him evermore. Then, for his sake, love all men, friends and foes, because they are his creation and image, and redeemed by Christ as you are. Search your minds for how you may do good to all men, as much as you have power, and hurt no man. Obey all your superiors and governors, serve your masters faithfully and diligently, in their absence as well as in their presence. Do not do it because of dread of punishment only, but for your conscience's sake, knowing that you are bound to do so by God's commandments. Do not disobey your fathers and mothers, but honour them, help them, and please them as much as you can. Do not oppress, do not kill, do not beat, do not slander nor hate any man. Love all men, speak well of all men, help and succour every man as you can—even your enemies who hate you, who speak evil of you, and who hurt you. Take no man's goods, nor covet your neighbour's goods wrongfully, but be content with what you have honestly. Give your own goods charitably, as need and situation requires. Flee all idolatry, witchcraft, and perjury. Commit no kind of adultery, fornication, nor other unchasteness, neither in will nor in deed, with any other man's wife, widow, maid or otherwise. And as you work continually during your life in observing the commandments of God (in which are found the pure, foremost, and direct honour of God, and which God has ordained to be the right way and pathway to heaven, if done in faith) you shall not fail, as Christ has promised, to come to that blessed and eternal life, where you will live in glory and joy with God forever. To him be praise, honour, and dominion, forever and ever. Amen.

 **matthias**media

Matthias Media is a ministry team of like-minded, evangelical Christians working together to achieve a particular goal, as summarized in our mission statement:

To serve our Lord Jesus Christ, and the growth of his gospel in the world, by producing and delivering high quality, Bible-based resources.

It was in 1988 that we first started pursuing this mission together, and in God's kindness we now have more than 250 different ministry resources being distributed all over the world. These resources range from Bible studies and books through to training courses and audio sermons.

To find out more about our large range of very useful products, and to access samples and free downloads, visit our website:

www.matthiasmedia.com.au

How to buy our resources

1. Direct from us over the internet:
   – in the US: www.matthiasmedia.com
   – in Australia and the rest of the world: www.matthiasmedia.com.au

2. Direct from us by phone:
   – in the US: 1 866 407 4530
   – in Australia: 1800 814 360 (Sydney: 9663 1478)
   – international: +61-2-9663-1478

3. Through a range of outlets in various parts of the world. Visit **www.matthiasmedia.com.au/international.php** for details about recommended retailers in your part of the world, including www.thegoodbook.co.uk in the United Kingdom.

4. Trade enquiries can be addressed to:
   – in the US: sales@matthiasmedia.com
   – in the UK: sales@ivpbooks.com
   – in Australia and the rest of the world: sales@matthiasmedia.com.au

The Implanted Word

8 studies on James, by Kirsten Birkett

Practicality. That's what Christians have always loved about James. It's a book about life in the real world—where the rich and poor struggle to get on, where there is as much suffering and sickness as joy, where Christians quarrel and fight and have a hard time controlling their tongues, and where we find ourselves compromised by becoming too friendly with the world. In a world like this, the key to survival and growth, says James, is to humbly receive the word which God has planted in us. And to receive it humbly means doing it.

The Implanted Word opens up the book of James in a fresh, interactive format that individuals and small groups will find easy to use.

FOR MORE INFORMATION OR TO ORDER, CONTACT:

Matthias Media
Telephone: +61-2-9663-1478
Facsimile: +61-2-9663-3265
Email: sales@matthiasmedia.com.au
www.matthiasmedia.com.au

Matthias Media (USA)
Ph: 1-866-407-4530
Fax: 724-964-8166
Email: sales@matthiasmedia.com
www.matthiasmedia.com